I0815454

# THE *Ramos* GIN FIZZ

# THE *Ramos* GIN FIZZ

JOHN SHELTON REED

LOUISIANA STATE UNIVERSITY PRESS
BATON ROUGE

Published by Louisiana State University Press
lsupress.org



Manufactured in the United States of America
First printing

Designer: Barbara Neely Bourgoyne
Typeface: Arno Pro
Printer and binder: Integrated Books International

Cover and frontispiece photograph by Sam Gregory Anselmo.

Cataloging-in-Publication Data are available from the Library of Congress.
ISBN 978-0-8071-8352-6 (cloth: alk. paper)

*To the immortal memory of*

*H. C. "Carl" Ramos,*

*publican and friend to man*

New Orleans is "the city of Mardi Gras, oysters Rockefeller, and the Ramos gin fizz."

—VICTOR BERNARD, *St. Louis Globe-Democrat,* 1943

New Orleans is "distinguished by superb cooking, an abominable climate, excellent manners, Creoles, gracious living, a widespread love of gambling, buoyant society, some of the best and also some of the worst architecture in the land, delicious odors, antiques dealers with a gift for extemporaneous story-telling, mockingbirds, Mardi Gras, the dominance of the Catholic religion, fine needlework, and the Ramos gin fizz."

—DAVID L. COHN, *New Orleans and Its Living Past,* 1941

New Orleans is "certainly one of the most civilized cities in the United States. Any town capable of producing shrimp remoulade, Louis Armstrong, and the Ramos Gin Fizz has nothing to apologize for."

—LEE ALLEN, *Cooperstown Corner,* 1969

# CONTENTS


Preface · xi

ONE The Ineffable Ramos Gin Fizz · 1

TWO Ramos the Man, 1858–1927 · 6

THREE Ramos the Fizz, 1919–Present · 35

FOUR Historical Interlude: The Kingfish Schools Some Yankees · 66

FIVE Ingredients · 75

SIX Techniques · 89

SEVEN Riffs, Spins, Takes, Twists, Plays, Etc. · 102

EIGHT Recipes · 110

Sources and Acknowledgments · 133

# PREFACE

This book comes as part of the Louisiana State University Press series Iconic Cocktails of New Orleans, and I count myself lucky to have drawn the Ramos Fizz. When I told people I was working on this book, eyebrows were raised. A whole book? About one cocktail? Ah, but no other cocktail has a history more interesting, a recipe more complex, a mystique more captivating. Thousands of words have been written just trying to *describe* it.

Writing this book has not been a tough job. My "research" required barhopping in New Orleans, rewarding conversations with genial bartenders, and a dozen or so attempts to make an acceptable Ramos at home. (I believe I have it now.) For other tasks I had the help of a great many people and institutions, whom I thank by name at the end of the book.

Three prefatory notes, since this is, after all, a preface:

People often refer to a Ramos Gin Fizz as a Ramos Fizz, or even simply a Ramos, and I do, too.

I have usually capitalized the names of cocktails, including the Ramos Gin Fizz, but when quoting others I have let their capitalization stand.

When talking about the drink or its inventor, Ramos is not pronounced RAH-mohs. Mr. Ramos and his family pronounced it RAY-mohs, and over time RAY-mus has become a common variant, probably to rhyme with "famous." Although it looks Hispanic or Portuguese, I suspect it is a corruption of the German surname Remus.

# THE Ramos GIN FIZZ

CHAPTER ONE

# The Ineffable Ramos Gin Fizz

The Ramos Gin Fizz is a cocktail from New Orleans that includes, among other things, lemon and lime juice, egg white, cream, and orange flower water. Shaken properly, it becomes a foamy white concoction that the *Kansas City Star* (1986) calls "the Crescent City's most notable contribution to civilized tippling." In the view of London's *Independent* newspaper (2005), the drink is "one of the aristocrats of the cocktail world." The *Esquire Drink Book* (1956) adds that "men of sensitive character approach this drink with uncovered heads as they would a rare old wine."

In 1895, when the drink was new on the scene, just a few years old, the *New Orleans Times-Democrat* raved about its "frothy delicacy, its quaint suggestion of fruit trees and summer odors, its evanescent flavors, blending like the hues of the rainbow, its cool, delicious whiteness, its sweet caresses as it wafts like an angel down the joyous throat." The article concluded, "All of these are things that no person can adequately describe"—but that hasn't stopped people from trying. They've said that the Ramos Gin Fizz is—

"like tangy liquid meringue with a gin hit,"
"a foamy, alcoholic orange creamsicle,"
"a sort of drinkable key lime pie,"
"heaven in a glass,"
"like drinking a flower,"
"a liquid cloud of joy,"
"ginny pillows of orange-blossomed delight,"
"decadent, floral, smooth as silk,"
"an Olympian soda-fountain drink,"
"humanity's nearest attempt yet at the ancients' ambrosia,"
"essence of angel feathers blended with whipped moonbeams."

OK, some folks do get carried away, but a Google search for juxtapositions of "Ramos Gin Fizz" and "ethereal" had 18,100 hits.

Bartenders often don't like to make a Ramos Fizz (for reasons we'll get to), but it's on the International Bartenders Association's online short list of "Unforgettables." *The Bachelor in New Orleans* (1942) called it a "fancy-pants of a tall drink," and cocktail historian David Wondrich wrote in *Esquire* (2007) that it is "fussy, dated, takes a long time to make and uses too many ingredients, one quite hard to find"—yet when the *International Review of Food & Wine* compiled a list of "Drinks: The World's Great Classics" in 1978, it was number one.

Wondrich thinks the Louisiana state legislature made a mistake in 2008 when it named the Sazerac the official cocktail of New Orleans. The Sazerac is a fine drink, to be sure, but he thinks the Ramos Fizz would have been a better choice. The Roosevelt Hotel's beverage manager, Russ Bergeron, agrees. (The Roosevelt's Sazerac Bar claims to serve about twenty thousand a year.) Bergeron argued, in *Imbibe* magazine (2018), that, as a brunch eye-opener and all-day pick-me-up, the Ramos represents his city's easy-going, good-timing culture better than the Sazerac.

It also evokes the Crescent City's mythic past. Although it was actually born in the unromantic business district of New Orleans, across Canal Street from the French Quarter, and first served to ordinary New South businessmen, not planters or riverboat gamblers, it has an antebellum aura. "To sip a Ramos Fizz on a hot day," Wondrich writes, "is to step into a sepia-toned world peopled with slim, brown-eyed beauties who smell of magnolias and freshly laundered linen, and tall, mustachioed gentlemen who never seem to work and will kill you if you ask them why."

Someone once said that the Ramos is like New Orleans itself: sweet and sour, a thing of froth and fizz, with an aroma of tropical fruit. As with the city, you may start out sipping it, yet somehow your glass is empty before you know it. And you want another.

Like most good things in New Orleans, the Ramos Fizz comes with a story.

CHAPTER TWO

# Ramos the Man, 1858–1927

The early history of the Ramos Fizz is inseparable from the biography of the man who invented it.

## ANCESTRY AND EARLY YEARS

Henry Charles Ramos was the son of German immigrants. Everyone called him Carl (German for Charles, of course), and sometimes he even signed his name that way. The German community of New Orleans in which he grew up was

The young H. C. Ramos. From *Southern Buck* (New Orleans Lodge No. 30, B.P.O.E. [Elks], 1907).

the largest in the South; in 1860 one out of every eight residents of the city was a German immigrant, and his parents were two of them. Carl's father came to New Orleans in the 1840s but moved with his wife to Vincennes, Indiana, shortly before Carl was born in 1856. Carl's brother William Otto was born there two years later, and a third son was born in 1860 in San Antonio. It seems as if the Ramoses were moving from one German American community to another; both Vincennes and San Antonio had large ones.

When the Civil War began, they were back in New Orleans, and Carl's father enlisted in the Confederate army. Although his obituary says that he "served throughout the long struggle," Confederate records indicate that he deserted when New Orleans fell to Union forces; if so, it was presumably to rejoin his wife and young children in the occupied city.

As a teenager Carl Ramos worked for a couple of beer halls in New Orleans owned by his landsmen Eugene Krost and Hugo Redwitz, then moved to Baton Rouge in 1876, where he took a job at an American-style bar and quickly acquired a reputation as a skilled bartender. Four years later he opened his own successful bar, the Capitol Saloon. In 1886 he sold that and, after trying his luck in Birmingham briefly, returned to New Orleans.

## THE IMPERIAL CABINET AND THE BIRTH OF THE FIZZ

In 1887 Ramos borrowed three thousand dollars from the woman he would marry the next year, Marianne Weishaar (née Meyer), the widow of a prosperous leather importer, and he and his brother William bought a saloon called the Imperial Cabinet. (Its previous owner, an Irishman named Pat Moran, represented Imperial Cabinet whiskey.) The business was at the intersection of Carondelet and Gravier Streets, on the ground floor of a four-story building, with a restaurant called Meyer's Table d'Hote Internationale on the floor above. The brothers kept the name Imperial Cabinet, but the sign out front said "Ramos," and that's what most people called it (although the *Times-Democrat* said that, for some reason, "the initiated" knew it as "the Bayou").

**H. C. RAMOS,**

**PROPRIETOR**

**IMPERIAL CABINET.**

**Fine Wines and Liquors.**

**40 - CARONDELET ST - 40**

**NEW ORLEANS.**

**Opposite the Cotton Exchange.**

**[dec19—8m]**

*Above:* Advertisement in the *Louisiana Review,* January 1889.

*Opposite:* Meyer's Table d'Hote Internationale [Ramos on ground floor]. From the collection of Chris McMillian.

MEYER'S
MEYER'S
RAMOS

The place was across the street from the New Orleans Cotton Exchange, and there were four other saloons in the same block, but Ramos's soon outshone the others. Its big attraction was a delightful drink that Carl had devised and originally called a New Orleans Gin Fizz. The date most often given for this invention is 1888, although there's reason to think it might have been later; in any case, by 1895 Ramos's saloon had become known as "the gin fizz place."

For the record, some have suggested that Ramos didn't actually invent the drink that bears his name. In 1942 a couple of Baton Rouge "old-timers" (unnamed) told a local newspaper that he was already serving it when he lived in Baton Rouge, and one of them claimed that he got his secret recipe from a friend named Philip Machet. This story was repeated by a Baton Rouge newspaperman in 1974 (with no evidence beyond "It is said"), and another Baton Rouge newsman claimed to have heard it in the 1960s from a New Orleans bartender (unnamed) and had it corroborated by "a now-deceased Baton Rouge historian" (also unnamed). My suspicion is that these folks just enjoyed claiming a New Orleans icon for their upriver hometown.

Ramos's claim that he invented the drink went unchallenged during his lifetime.

Whoever invented it and whenever he did it, a writer in the *Birmingham News* recalled in 1927 that Ramos's Fizz immediately made the Imperial Cabinet "hardly less than a shrine" for the city's cotton brokers, and soon other men "engaged in the world's work there—bankers, lawyers, physicians, importers, contractors, realtors and newspapermen—" became regulars. A reporter for the local *Times-Democrat* wrote in 1897 of the saloon's "atmosphere of strangely admixtured hustling and luxury. Before the bar stands a row of well-dressed gentlemen languidly sipping the nectarious concoctions for which the place is so famous, while behind the bar the barkeepers leap round with the energy of crickets," all overseen by Carl Ramos, "a man of immense and unremitting energy, always genial, obliging, courteous and merry."

Ramos promoted his business by giving away small leather wallets and lucky penny holders inscribed with his name and "Gin Fizz—Gin Phizz!" Soon his saloon became a tourist attraction: by 1895 the *Times-Democrat* said it was known "among men of the world throughout the United States." In 1899 *Leslie's Weekly* reported that "visitors to New Orleans who want to 'see the sights' are always taken to H. C. Ramos's place," where "patrons stand around the little room three deep waiting for a chance to be served." By that time Ramos was using the whites of five thousand eggs a week (supplied by "the largest hennery in the country"), which implies that he was using some thirteen thousand bottles of gin a year.

If business was booming in ordinary times, in the winter tourist season and during Carnival it exploded. A *Times-Democrat* reporter wrote in 1897 that then, "it is all

Penny holder. Courtesy of Bruce Perdue, encasedcoins.info.

Henry Ramos can do to supply the demand for gin fizzes. From the hotels come white-aproned waiters with silver trays, bearing orders for one or two or half dozen of the delicious concoctions; from the clubs of Canal Street come messengers; from the offices of brokers, from the palatial sanctums of merchants; fevered persons tossing upon their beds crave of their physicians the boon of a cool and grateful fizz from Ramos."

## ABOUT THOSE SHAKER BOYS

Almost from the beginning Ramos employed "shaker boys" to do the menial labor of shaking his Fizzes. In 1899, according to *Leslie's Weekly,* one was assigned to each of Ramos's eight bartenders; later, a platoon of shaker boys served all the bartenders. A bartender would hand a drink to a shaker boy, who would shake it and pass it on to the next, who would shake it and pass it on in turn.

Lately there has been some misunderstanding about who the shaker boys were. One YouTube authority, for instance, tells us that they were "children who were paid a dollar a shake"; another that Ramos "had to hire hundreds of kids to hide behind the restaurant to shake this drink up." Sadly, though, no one familiar with the argot of white Southerners in the Jim Crow era will be surprised to learn that the "shaker boys" were actually African American men—and not necessarily young.

Stanley Clisby Arthur wrote in *Famous New Orleans Drinks and How to Mix 'Em* (1938) that Ramos's "corps of busy shaker boys behind the bar were one of the sights of the town during Carnival." And no wonder: they put on a show. In a nostalgic letter to the *Tampa Tribune* in 1930 one old-timer recalled that they "did nothing but shake the delirious concoction into a soap-sudsy mass of white foam," but he recognized that there was skill involved: "It was a delight just to see those boys, in their spotlessly white aprons, deftly mixing and churning your glass of fizz. They never stopped their movements until the fizz was ready for your palate. And they knew to a certainty just when the cocktail was ready. Never too soon, and never too late—but just so. Then they poured it out quickly and surely.

Shaker boys as imagined in *Irwin S. Cobb's Own Recipe Book* (1934). Copyright © 1934 by Frankfort Distilleries, Louisville and Baltimore.

. . . Ramos' boys were particular about the way they mixed and served those gin fizzes." He added, "For a few pennies they would dance a jig in time to the swing of their arms."

In 2007 the authors of *In the Land of Cocktails* put together a more diverse set of shaker boys (and some girls) as a sort of tribute act to promote their book. In the 2020s, the Fabulous Shaker Boys, a cocktail catering business in Amsterdam, also pays homage to the New Orleans originals, and a cocktail-themed juggling act in Berlin called "The Shaker Boys" may do the same.

## FORTUNE AND LOCAL FAME

Ramos's business made him a rich man. In 1911 a visitor from Montana wrote in his hometown *Fergus County Democrat,* "From the mob that surged and swayed before his bar it occurred to me that if Ramos hoped to get all the money in Louisiana, I couldn't see where anybody had a chance to beat him to it."

Marianne, two years older than Carl, had two young children when she and Carl married; later, the couple would have two of their own. The family lived in an elegant antebellum Italianate townhouse on North Rampart Street, facing "Beauregard" (Congo) Square, featured later in the *Sunday Picayune* as one of the "handsome homes of New Orleans." (These days Ramos Fizzes are on the menu of a "craft bar" in the next block.)

Eventually Ramos acquired all the accoutrements of New Orleans haute bourgeois life. He became a regular subscriber to the French Opera and joined the Southern Yacht Club. He bought a summer home on ten acres in Covington, with a keeper's lodge and pecan and fruit trees.

He entered a horse in the 1900 Horse Show, and his collie took first in class at the State Fair Dog Show. In 1905 the Ramos family vacationed in Havana, and in 1912 he bought a Cadillac.

Although his father and brother William were practicing Catholics, he seems to have had no church affiliation. He was a Master Mason, though, and one of the several affiliated Masonic orders to which he belonged was the Knights Templar, which requires its members to profess a belief in Christianity. He was also a member of the Elks Club, which had a large and active New Orleans lodge.

Ramos's business made him not just rich, but famous. As early as 1891 the *Louisiana Review* referred to him as "Carl Ramos, clever Carl, the genial and universally popular proprietor of that tip top saloon, the Imperial Cabinet." Soon he was being called "prince of New Orleans barkeepers, . . . the most expert mixologist of the South." By 1903 his fame was such that when the *Times-Picayune* printed a photo of him taken from behind and challenged readers to "Guess Who This Is," the list of those who answered correctly filled three columns of small type.

The bar at the Stag [Ramos at left]. From the collection of Chris McMillian.

As a dedicated Freemason, Ramos wasn't an obvious candidate for a place in cocktail history. Like most Masons at the time, he strongly disapproved of drunkenness, and he didn't tolerate it in his bar. Although he drank wine at home, he never drank at work. He closed his bar no later than 11:00 p.m., and many evenings at 8:00 p.m. He opened on Sunday only from 11:00 to 12:00 p.m. and from 4:30 to 5:30 p.m.—and that only because his customers begged him to. It would be a stretch to suggest that he created the Ramos Fizz as a temperance drink, but there are certainly easier ways to drink too much. A widespread story too good to be true has it that when the hatchet-wielding "saloon wrecker" Carrie Nation came to New Orleans, she said that Prohibition wouldn't be needed if everyone who served liquor was like Mr. Ramos.

In 1907, when the Imperial Cabinet's landlord raised his rent to five hundred dollars, Ramos poor-mouthed to the *Item* newspaper, "I could not pay anything like that. I've been here twenty years and I have an established business, but there is not that much money in it." He, his brother William, and their head bartender and partner Paul Alpuente bought the Stag Saloon and a four-year lease on its building from Ramos's brother Elk Tom Anderson (whose many business interests had earned him the unofficial title "Mayor of Storyville"—New Orleans's red-light district). All of the contents of the Imperial Cabinet were sold at auction, including a "Magnificent Hand-Carved English Oak Sideboard, originally costing a small fortune."

## THE STAG SALOON AND NATIONAL RENOWN

The Stag, around the corner and down the block from the Imperial Cabinet, was an elegant place with tile floors, the longest bar in the city, and six elk heads mounted on the wall. A large illuminated sign with green letters spelling out "Gin Fizz / Ramos" went up out front, and locals called this new place, like the old, simply "Ramos." The move made Ramos even more successful than he had been at the old location. In 1915 he and his partners bought the building.

The volume of business at the Stag is hard to imagine. Looking back, Paul Alpuente told the *Item* in 1933 that "it was often that we used as many as eight or ten cases of eggs a day." At 360 eggs to a case, that works out to hundreds of thousands of Gin Fizzes a year. The number of bartenders and shaker boys grew proportionately. Alpuente remembered nineteen bartenders at Carnival season; ordinarily there were twenty or so shaker boys at work, but reportedly on Mardi Gras in 1915 there were thirty-five. All of this was under the eye of the imperturbable proprietor, with (the *Item* newspaper recalled in 1925) "his ruddy face and genial blue eyes sparkling behind silver rimmed, ear bowed spectacles, his snowy hair, his pure white shirt with a diamond in its bosom, his short, stout frame."

Ramos's business occasionally had hiccups. His practice of freely cashing customers' checks was greatly appreciated—one Saturday night he reportedly cashed twenty-two thousand dollars' worth—but sometimes one bounced and he had to wait for it to be made good. He was arrested and fined twenty-five dollars in 1907, when the Stag was one of seven saloons caught up in a sweep for violations of the Sunday closing law, despite its limited Sunday hours. A more serious problem arose when Ramos was one of three prominent liquor-license holders sued by the state in 1905 for underreporting their receipts (the others were the city's exclusive Chess, Checkers and Whist Club and Lulu White, madam of a famous Storyville brothel). Ramos was accused of reporting less than a third of his sales and was ordered to pay the amount he had underpaid, plus interest—nearly two hundred thousand dollars

HAVE YOU EVER TASTED

—THE—

ORIGINAL RAMOS

Gin Fizz?

The NECTAR of NEW ORLEANS

Delicious

Cool--Inspiring

THE PLACE IS "**THE STAG,**" 712-714 GRAVIER STREET, OPPOSITE THE SAINT CHARLES HOTEL, - NEW ORLEANS, LA.

***YOU'LL NOT FORGET IT WHEN YOU'VE ONCE BEEN THERE.***

"The Nectar of New Orleans." From the collection of Chris McMillian.

in today's money. But even this was only a temporary setback.

At the Imperial Cabinet, Ramos had maintained a little side room where ladies could come with their escorts in the busy winter season and be served, but the Stag, as its name implies, was a male preserve. Women were allowed only on Mardi Gras day. In fact, in 1908 the Louisiana legislature made even that illegal—alcohol could be sold to women only in restaurants—but in New Orleans on Mardi Gras nobody paid much attention to that. Other times of the year it was a common practice for ladies to wait in the carriage—later, in the car—for their escorts to bring them a Gin Fizz. And when a visiting couple from Detroit ran into the no-women rule, they made a pitiful plea to Ramos, who told them to come to the alley door at closing time. He met them there, gave each a Gin Fizz, and refused to take payment.

Ramos's gift for promotion flourished in the Stag era. In 1911 he sent Paul Alpuente to mix Fizzes in Washington to help New Orleans's effort to secure the Panama Canal exposition (although, in the event, it went to San Francisco). In 1907 Alpuente had gone to Chicago to fix drinks for thirsty Shriners at their national convention, while in 1910, according to the *Detroit Times,* Ramos himself took "a corps of clerks and assistants, together with two baggage cars full of ingredients and equipment" to serve the Elks' convention in Detroit. Presumably conventioneers from all over the country went home licking their lips, and spread the word.

The national reputations of Carl Ramos, his Fizz, and his saloon were already considerable; these efforts extended them. Alderman Sidney Story (best known now as the namesake of Storyville) wrote in *Beverages De Luxe* (1914), "No beverage of recent years has drawn to itself more praise and attention than the 'Ramos Gin Fizz.' . . . The glories and reputation of this Ambrosial drink have been sung the world over." In 1917, the *Brownsville (Texas) Herald* said it was as famous as Elinor Glyn's *Three Weeks* (a best-selling erotic novel), and a letter to the *New York Sun* provided a supposed recipe (more accurate than most) "for such as cannot make the trip to New Orleans." In 1919 a writer in the *Raleigh News and Observer* claimed he had "never met a much traveled person of either sex who had not visited Ramos' place in New Orleans."

---

When E. C. Miller, president of the American Photo-Engravers Association, visited New Orleans in 1919, some friends who went to see him at his hotel reported that "Miller was in the bath-tub with a Sazerac cocktail in one hand, a Ramos gin fizz in the other and a Ojen cocktail in his shaving cup. He seemed to become acclimated almost immediately."

---

The Ramos Fizz was so much a part of the national conversation that references to it didn't have to be explained. An Atlanta sportswriter could quip in 1913 that the Georgia Tech football team's "offensive strength is as unknown as the component parts of a Ramos gin fizz." When Warren Harding visited New Orleans the year after Prohibition began, the *Tampa Tribune* commented, "Think of what Mr. Harding missed by not striking New Orleans in the day of the late famous 'Ramos fizz!'"

## CIVIC LIFE AND THE END OF THE SALOON

Ramos had other business interests; he bought and sold commercial real estate, represented some patent medicines, invested in an oil drilling company, and became secretary treasurer of a Red Rock Ginger Ale distributor. He was active in a businessmen's organization called the Progressive Union, helped to organize the Louisiana Retail Liquor Dealers' Association, and served as the first president of the Louisiana Anti-Prohibition League.

He was a longtime member of the Choctaw Club (the New Orleans version of the Democratic Party's Tammany Hall in New York) and supported various municipal improvements and projects. New Orleans newspapers were filled with notices of his charitable and civic activities. He served as president of the board of directors of the Milne Asylum for Destitute Orphan Boys. He gave to Touro Infirmary and Charity Hospital, to the Michel Heyman Free Kindergarten and the Louisiana SPCA, to the Young Men's Gymnastic Club, the Young Men's Hebrew Association, and the Confederate Reunion Fund. He gave to fight yellow fever, to promote tourism, and to support victims of a volcano eruption in Martinique. He had been a volunteer fireman and remained active in the Firemen's Charitable and Benevolent Association. And this is just a partial list.

In 1914 he received the ultimate Southern honorific when Alderman Story referred to "the genial and courtly proprietor of the 'Stag,' Col. H. C. Ramos." (Imagine: "Colonel Ramos.") But Ramos's local eminence ultimately rested on his saloon, and it became increasingly obvious that Prohibition was coming and the saloon's days were numbered. The future of the Ramos Fizz was the subject of much speculation; it was rumored, for instance, that Ramos was going to open a bar in Bermuda. But that was just a rumor. He stayed in New Orleans and took defeat gracefully.

Prohibition went into effect on January 17, 1920. There's a legend that as midnight approached on January 16, Ramos made a valedictory Gin Fizz, served it, and closed his bar with the words, "I've sold my last Gin Fizz." But the reality was more prosaic. Faced with inevitable closing,

BY ALBERT L. PAUL BY ALBERT L. PAUL BY ALBERT L. PAUL

**Magnificent Fixtures, Equipment and Paintings**

**of the Famous H. C. Ramos, Ltd.**

**"STAG SALOON"**

**The Home of the Original Gin Fizz**

**No. 712 Gravier Street**

**On Wednesday, August 20, 1919, at 11 A. M.**

**Comprising**

Elegant Mahogany Bar Fixtures and Counters Costing $6000.00.

The Historical Picture of the Old Metairie Race Course, Portraying Numerous Celebrities, by W. P. Moise.

The Famous Painting of "Diana After the Chase."

Four National cash registers, one costing $850.00, and registers from 1 cent to $9999.00, expensive solid mahogany office partitions, electric fans, mahogany settees, chairs, tables, iron safe, oyster counter, lunch counter, mirrors, roll-top desks, steel engravings, large assortment of silverware, crockery, glasses and glassware, range, trucks, cigar stand, show cases, ice crushers, brass cuspidors, electric beer pump, and the beautiful art glass canopy, 50 feet long in front, and numerous other articles.

Terms cash.

ALBERT L. PAUL, Auctioneer.

Aug. 17-18-19-20.

BY STERN'S AUCTION EXCHANGE

The Stag's furnishings at auction. *New Orleans Times-Picayune,* August 1919.

Ramos had shut his doors more than five months earlier, saying that he did not want to violate the law in any way. The Stag's six elk heads went to adorn New Orleans's grand Elks Lodge, Ramos kept a fancy clock for himself, and the rest of the furnishings were sold at auction in August 1919. The results were disappointing: A painting Ramos had once been offered $3,400 for was sold for $850. The huge mahogany and glass bar fixture, valued at $6,000, went for $200 to adorn a soft drink stand in Columbia, Mississippi. In the end, the furnishings realized less than 20 percent of their valuation, but the *Times-Picayune* reported that "every single little trifle was sold, down to odd spoons, to be kept as a remembrance of probably the best-known saloon on the globe."

The next day a headline appeared in the *Memphis News-Scimitar:* "Ramos' Gin Fizz Palace closed forever and fixtures auctioned yesterday. What will be the use of ever going to New Orleans again?"

## LIFE AND DEATH IN FORCED RETIREMENT

Carl's brother William bought a paint company and began making and selling "Jinn Phizz" paint; Carl may have been an investor, but he wasn't an officer or involved in the day-to-day running of the firm. Reporters who interviewed him in 1925 said that he reminisced about "the good old days when the Ramos establishment was synonymous with New Orleans and a show place of the city." He told about his trips to London and Paris and Dublin, boasted that his bartenders had included a German nobleman and Charles Ponzi of the original Ponzi scheme, and recalled the time he had twenty-two congressmen and eight governors lined up at his bar. "I went as a private individual to the world fairs in Chicago, St. Louis and Paris," he said. "Though I made no claim, everywhere I found myself pointed out as the Ramos of New Orleans." But overnight he had gone from being a respected and celebrated public figure, at the heart of the city's civic life, to being just another nostalgic old-timer. "I wish I were back," he said. "I was in my glory then."

And he had other reasons to be dejected. After his teenaged daughter Stella died in 1916, his marriage deteriorated; by 1925 he was estranged from his wife, Marianne, his two stepchildren, and his son Carl E. Ramos. He may have felt some financial strain as well. In any case, he sold his grand house on North Rampart Street and bought a smaller place uptown. Two years later Marianne left home

H. C. Ramos in his late sixties. *New Orleans Item*, August 1925.

and filed for separation. An unpleasant suit followed, with nasty charges and countercharges, before she was awarded alimony and a division of property.

When Ramos died in 1928, *Time* magazine took note. An Associated Press obituary was printed in dozens of newspapers nationwide: in California, the *Santa Maria*

*Daily Times* headlined it, "Famous Barkeeper Dead." A Saint Louis paper paid tribute by reprinting his Fizz recipe (which he had finally shared with the public in 1925). The hometown *Times-Picayune* hailed him as "famous throughout the civilized world as the originator of the Ramos gin fizz," and the *Item* said, "He was respected throughout America, not only as the originator of the delectable drink, but as a type of exemplary saloonkeeper, a genial, generous host, and a man who never drank." (This last was part of his legend, if not quite true.)

After a Masonic funeral held at the Scottish Rite Cathedral, a five-minute walk from his old saloons, he was buried in Metairie Cemetery, with his daughter Stella. Each year during Tales of the Cocktail, an annual trade conference and festival in New Orleans, a group of bartenders visits his grave.

His will divided his surprisingly modest estate equally among his brother William, his brother Joseph Edward's widow, and a trust for his son Carl.

CHAPTER THREE

# Ramos the Fizz, 1919–Present

With Ramos forced into retirement and sharing his secret recipe with the world, the Ramos Gin Fizz took on a life of its own. It did not begin well.

## THE PROHIBITION YEARS

Prohibition didn't quite work as planned, but it did effectively stop the consumption of the Ramos Fizz in the United States, even in New Orleans.

New Orleanians didn't stop drinking—far from it. Local socialite and preservationist Elizebeth Werlein once counted seventy-four bars in nine blocks of the French Quarter. You could get a drink in a teacup at Arnaud's, a bottle from an Italian corner grocery, a five-gallon keg of Cuban grain alcohol from a fisherman. William Faulkner got his liquor from a priest at the cathedral. If you were willing to pay enough, you could get a decent cocktail made with good liquor, but most Prohibition-era drinkers wanted something with more kick than a Ramos Fizz. They took their spirits neat or with only the most rudimentary mixers (often chosen to mask the taste of bathtub gin or "Scotch straight off the boat"). In 1927 a *Times-Picayune* columnist wrote that a popular little book called *Here's How* offered recipes for concoctions "calculated to prove as effective as knock-out drops," adding, "What a falling-off there from the days of the Ramos gin fizz, the Sazerac, the mint julep!" (And it didn't help the Ramos that elaborate cocktails were more difficult to conceal in the event of a raid.) So even in the city of its birth the Ramos Fizz was driven not just underground but almost out of existence.

At least four racehorses and one racing greyhound have been named Ramos Fizz.

In some places abroad, however, it survived and even flourished. American tourists in France could quench their Ramos thirst at Harry's New York Bar in Paris, the New York Bar in Nice, or the Bristol Bar in Beaulieu-sur-Mer. The Ramos was the specialty of the house at the Hotel International in Panama City, thanks to an expatriate New Yorker named McEwen. The famous barman Harry Craddock, another refugee from New York, would mix you one at the Savoy Hotel in London. The *New Orleans Item* reported that "returning travelers say fair imitations [of classic New Orleans cocktails] are dispensed by former New Orleans bartenders in Hong King, Manila and Havana." (Recipe collections from Havana's El Floridita and Sloppy Joe's both included the Ramos Fizz.) Other sources sprang up just across the Canadian and Mexican borders: the Hotel Vancouver, a bar in Tiajuana, the Kentucky Club in Juarez, and famously at the Cadillac Bar in Nuevo Laredo.

## A BRIEF EXCURSION SOUTH OF THE BORDER

In 1926 a New Orleanian named Achilles Mehault "Mayo" Bessan bought a bar just across the Rio Grande from Laredo, Texas. After a change of name and location, his Cadillac Bar in Nuevo Laredo became what the *New York Times* called "the best run and most delightful watering hole" on the border. With parrots and monkeys in the parking lot, gambling in the back room, a menu in English, and prices in dollars, the Cadillac was a legendary gathering place for day-tripping Texans and other Americans looking to escape the strictures of Prohibition. "Big Daddy" Bessan never needed to learn Spanish, and never did.

Drawing on his Louisiana heritage, Bessan offered a delicious mix of Mexican and New Orleans dishes—fresh seafood, turtle soup, and renowned frog legs—but what went on the sign outside was "Home of Famous Ramos Gin Fizz."

Bessan's bona fides were in order. He had worked for Carl Ramos in the old days and replicated the Ramos

Cadillac Bar, Nuevo Laredo. Courtesy of Wanda Garner Cash.

recipe and the Ramos experience, complete with multiple bartenders and attendant "shaker boys." The Cadillac became the best-known purveyor of Ramos Gin Fizzes outside New Orleans and remained that until 1949, when the Roosevelt Hotel challenged its use of the trademarked name (see page 49). Bessan changed the name of the drink his bar was famous for to "New Orleans Gin Fizz" (the original name, anyway), but, he said, "The recipe's still the Ramos original"—and everyone knew it.

Bessan died in 1969, and the bar's ownership passed out of the family a decade later, but the Cadillac remained a South of the Border institution until the turn of the century. It finally closed its doors in 2010.

## FROM REPEAL TO DISCO

The Ramos may have been mostly a memory in New Orleans during Prohibition, but it was a loving and robust memory, so it came back strong after Repeal in 1933. In fact, drinkers started celebrating on the day the last of the required state ratifications passed, a month before Repeal was official. The next morning an Associated Press story reported that "the Ramos gin fizz and Sazerac cocktail were readily available in old New Orleans [and] there appeared to be no attempt on the part of local authorities to act against those who have jumped the repeal gun." Four days later the *New Orleans States* observed, "The Ramos Gin Fizz is the most popular of all the drinks served over the bar at this writing."

Most things quickly returned to pre-Prohibition normal. Before 1919 any white male visiting New Orleans had been almost required to drink a Ramos Fizz at Carl Ramos's saloon: in 1936 the *Indianapolis Star* recalled that "it was not uncommon for travellers to visit Ramos' famous establishment as soon as they arrived in New Orleans and before they registered at hotels." Once again, after Repeal, syndicated columnist George Tucker wrote, "you must order a Ramos gin fizz the moment you arrive in New Orleans, even before you check into your hotel." He said, "It's just one of those things, like tossing your lei into the sunset when you leave Honolulu."

Women's progress, as illustrated by John Held Jr. in a 1935 recipe book. Courtesy of Sazerac Archives.

One thing had changed, though: Prohibition had largely done away with the strictures on women drinking in public. Although many old-line hotel bars still maintained a men-only policy, speakeasies had been more easygoing about it and stayed that way when they became legal drinking establishments.

The drink's fame was again nationwide. Anyone who might have forgotten was reminded when Senator Huey Long made it national news in 1935 (see chapter 4). An *Oakland Tribune* reporter wrote in 1941, "At last count, before I hopped aboard the Lark [train to New Orleans], exactly 878 Oakland citizens asked me to drink a Ramos Fizz for them on New Year's Eve." Sportswriters could once again deploy similes like "Connie Mack shook the A's lineup as violently as a bartender shaking a Ramos fizz" (*Philadelphia Inquirer,* 1935).

In the public mind the Ramos became associated with celebrity, sophistication, and glamour. It turned up on newspapers' society pages and in gossip columns and movie magazines. Aaron Pringle, bartender and movie critic at Avocado.com, says that when Humphrey Bogart's

Lizabeth Scott and Humphrey Bogart in *Dead Reckoning* (1947). Copyright © 1947, renewed 1974 Columbia Pictures Industries, Inc. All Rights Reserved. Courtesy of Columbia Pictures.

leading lady Lizabeth Scott ordered a Ramos Fizz in the 1947 film noir *Dead Reckoning,* "audiences would have recognized . . . a refined classy cocktail favored by high society types," so her order "shorthands that she has taste, experience, and money." It could also convey a whiff of decadence: playboy Porfirio Rubirosa and playwright

Portrait of Tennessee Williams in the Mississippi Hall of Fame. Collection of the Museum Division, Mississippi Department of Archives and History. Used by permission.

Tennessee Williams both ordered it regularly. (Williams's portrait in the Mississippi Hall of Fame in Jackson shows him with his ever-present Ramos and an ashtray from the Carousel Bar at the Monteleone Hotel.)

The Ramos was at home in nightclubs: bandleader Harry James, torch singer Julie London, and jazzman Charles Mingus were all seen with one in hand. It was a favorite of the Algonquin Round Table veteran Heywood Broun and of sportswriter Grantland Rice. *The Field Guide to Drinking in America* (2015) reports that Frank Sinatra was introduced to the Ramos Fizz as a hangover cure by Robert Mitchum, who said that it "goes down like mother's milk." (Grateful for the tip, Sinatra nicknamed Mitchum "Mother" and sent him cards on Mother's Day.) Sinatra biographer Bill Zehme says that Ol' Blue Eyes ordered Ramoses sent in bulk to the Sands steam room, where he passed them around to his Rat Pack pals, and he paid tribute to the drink in the movie *Ocean's 11* when his character talks about using the money from a Las Vegas heist to buy out the Miss Universe contest "and just sit around and talk to the girls, one by one. Find out how things are in Sweden. Or invite them for a weekend to New Orleans. Ramos gin fizzes, oysters Rockefeller . . ."

At midcentury the Ramos Fizz was firmly established in the cocktail equivalent of the Great American Songbook. There's a widely accepted if not entirely accurate story about what happened after that, but first—

## AN ASIDE ON TRADEMARK ENFORCEMENT

Two days after Prohibition ended, Ramos's widow and children set up "H. C. Ramos, Ltd., Incorporated" and moved to register the trade names "Ramos Gin Fizz" and "Ramos." Four months later an ad in the *Times-Picayune* proclaimed that the "Original and Only Ramos' Gin Fizz" could be found "Exclusively at Hotel Roosevelt Bars." Fine print under the word "Ramos'" warned, "Trademark Registered." The Roosevelt's Blue Room began to advertise that it was "The Exclusive Home of the Original and ONLY Ramos' Gin Fizz," and the corporation began to line up "exclusive homes" in other cities.

The next year, in 1935, the corporation reached an agreement with Seymour Weiss, owner of the Roosevelt (and consigliere to Huey Long), that the Roosevelt could han-

Roosevelt Hotel, ca. 1941. Screen capture from Internet Archive: Home Movies: Summers collection: New Orleans to San Francisco, ca. 1941.

dle the franchising and enforce the trademark. Soon the cocktail list at the Hotel New Yorker in Manhattan offered a Ramos Gin Fizz for forty-five cents and bragged that the drink was "Obtainable in New York only at the Hotel

New Yorker." A Dayton newspaper ad suggested, "Lower the Temperature with a Smooth and Potent Ramos Gin Fizz. Offered exclusively at the Hotel Van Cleve." Hotels in Chicago, Cleveland, and San Francisco also paid monthly fees for exclusive franchises, and no one was more into it than the Lincoln Hotel in Indianapolis, which offered "the original, genuine Ramos Fizz" at a special introductory price and brought in "Roscoe, a Negro bar attendant from New Orleans and a specialist in shaking and serving the fizz, [who] will enliven the proceedings and greatly increase patrons' enjoyment of this old favorite."

Word got out. A columnist in the *Washington Post* wrote, "Another tip to those who have heard of the Ramos gin fizz, popular in New Orleans and protected by copyright, and all that sort of thing. Ask the waiter for a New Orleans gin fizz. They are remarkably similar."

Although enforcement of the trademark seems to have been fitful, the Roosevelt did come down on the Cadillac Bar in Nuevo Laredo in 1949. As late as 1968 the Ramos corporation lawyer was telling the *States-Item* that the authentic Ramos Gin Fizz could be found in New Orleans only at the Roosevelt, and warning visitors not to drink "an imitation with a misleading name, which would only resemble the real drink as the mist resembles the rain," and in 1979 the Fairmont Hotel in San Francisco was still paying something on the order of one hundred dollars a month for the right to call its gin fizz "Ramos" (although scores of other California restaurants were advertising their unlicensed Ramos Fizz brunches—see below). Soon after, the New Orleans Fairmont (formerly the Roosevelt) terminated its agreement with the Ramos company, and even sporadic enforcement ceased.

## THE DARK AGE OF COCKTAIL CULTURE

The story has it that, starting around 1970, the Ramos Fizz went into eclipse almost everywhere (except New Orleans, of course, where it was never forgotten), and it's true that, to some extent, *all* of America's classic cocktails did. David Wondrich argues that this was part of a more general rejection of tradition, as mainstream America assimilated the values of the 1960s counterculture. Many young people rejected their parents' alcohol buzz and got their kicks from marijuana and psychedelics, while those who did imbibe turned to sweet, colorful, insipid drinks, often with naughty names. A spokesperson for National Distillers was quoted in the *New York Post* as saying, "The baby-boomers have a sweet tooth and want instant gratification." A collective failure of taste led to things like the Harvey Wallbanger and the Fuzzy Navel. Writing in the *New York Times* in 2012, Robert Simonson called the 1970s and 1980s "the cocktail doldrums . . . when vodka swamped the American bar scene and sloppy disco drinks all but obliterated sophisticated tippling."

In his 2016 book *A Proper Drink,* Simonson does acknowledge that a light flared briefly in this darkness: oddly enough, at the bar and restaurant chain TGI Fridays. In the late 1970s Fridays was primarily a singles bar, designed to attract the young of both sexes (the word "yuppie" dates from about this time), and the chain's bartenders were required to complete an intensive nine-month training program that included some instruction in mixing classic cocktails. One result was that Ramos Fizzes were being served in places like Memphis, Little Rock, Tampa, and Dallas. In 1979 Fridays in Phoenix, Orlando, and West Des Moines advertised them in local newspapers; Fridays in Nashville had them for ninety-five cents. But when a change in ownership in 1983 reduced the training program from nine months to six weeks, the light was extinguished, and the field was left to the sloppy disco drinks. Simonson says that the 1980s were "a time when few people outside New Orleans knew what a Ramos Fizz was."

But it's not quite that simple. To be sure, in the bars of American cities, where single young people gathered and bartending careers were made or broken, the Ramos Fizz had become an antiquated relic, if it was remembered at all. In those settings, as John Egerton wrote in 1993, in his magisterial *Southern Food,* "the Sazerac and the Ramos Gin Fizz . . . are now more historical curiosities than popular libations." But elsewhere the Ramos Fizz was more popular than ever, just with a different demographic, and not in bars, but in restaurants and backyards.

## THE GOLDEN STATE RAMOS FIZZ

On May 19, 1954, an ad for the Capitol Inn in the *Sacramento Bee* offered "the Famous New Orleans Ramos Fizz" and added, "Come for Brunch!" This is the earliest reference I've found to what would eventually become an internationally famous institution, the California Ramos Fizz brunch. It was slow to start, but the pace picked up in the 1960s; by 1989 more than a hundred California restaurants had paid to advertise their Ramos Fizz brunches, and presumably many more who had them didn't advertise. Sam's Anchor Café in Tiburon, the Alta Mira Hotel in Sausalito, Rosie's in Tahoe City, the Cliff House and Lehr's Greenhouse in San Francisco—these and others established traditions that lasted for years (in a few cases even to this day).

But the Ramos wasn't just for brunch. Some restaurants simply advertised it without specifying when it was available, and one in Petaluma bragged, "Any Day—Any Time." And it wasn't just for restaurants. Newspapers began to report its presence at meetings, fundraisers, civic club picnics, and especially at parties in people's homes.

Now Featuring

The Famous New Orleans

RAMOS FIZZ

in the New Pacifica Room

COME FOR BRUNCH!

—NOW PLAYING—

SAL CARSON

And His Band

BILL PANELL

AND HIS ORCHESTRA

RETURN

June 8TH!

Let us help you plan your
banquets and parties
NEVER A COVER CHARGE

GI 2-0481

SOPHISTICATED
PEOPLE
ENJOY THE
RAMOS FIZZ
BREAKFAST
EVERY SUNDAY MORNING
AT THE
HACIENDA

8 A.M.-
11 A.M.
$2.00

HACIENDA
HIGHWAY 99 & CLINTON
PH. AM 8-4061

*Above:* Ad for a Ramos Fizz breakfast. *Fresno Bee*, February 1968.

*Left:* Ramos Fizz brunch advertised in the *Sacramento Bee*, May 1954.

Suggested party menus and accounts of fancy social events mentioned the drink; ads for grocery and liquor stores included recipes. Not only were there parties where Ramos Fizzes were served, there were *Ramos Fizz parties,* where the occasion was about the drink.

To be sure, recipes used at these events could be peculiar. The *Pasadena Star News* suggested replacing the original recipe's cream, egg white, and vanilla with vanilla ice cream—a "sneaky shortcut" sent in by a reader ("Clever gal, that one!"). The *Sacramento Bee*'s Ramos Fizz was made with brandy, a whole egg, and bitters, while the *Los Angeles Times* offered one that called for gin "or, if you prefer, bourbon" and another that included "orange juice, half-and-half and tequila." Whatever these were, they weren't Ramos *Gin* Fizzes.

---

In 1964 the 7 Up company published a booklet entitled *Great Drinks Made Simple.* Its recipe for a "Ramoz [*sic*] Gin Fizz" substituted 7 Up for seltzer.

---

Other odd recipes turned up in community cookbooks compiled by social clubs and civic institutions. One from the Inglewood, California, hospital auxiliary included orange juice and lemonade frozen concentrates and a whole egg. (That orange juice often substituted for hard-to-get orange flower water. In fact, a Safeway supermarket ad said that Minute Maid frozen concentrate "Makes a Good Ramos Fizz." It certainly made the hostess's life easier. Presumably the "Ramos Fizz Mix" advertised by Mar Vista Market did, too.)

Eventually many Californians came to see the Ramos Fizz as a fashionable feature of home entertainment, even as part of the California lifestyle, like the backyard barbecue pit. "Everyone drinks Ramos gin fizz in San Francisco," *Courvoisier's Book of the Best* remarked in 1988. "It's a very West Coast brunchtime drink." In 1985 the Pottery Barn in Los Angeles advertised a "Classic Adirondack Chair" with "Wide flat arms to hold Ramos gin fizz, binoculars, and volume III of Remembrance of Things Past."

The Ramos Fizz brunch was always predominantly a California thing. Over 90 percent of newspaper ads for it in the 1960s were in California papers. But in this as in so many respects, other places followed California's example. Although a majority of advertisements in the 1980s were still from California papers, the Ramos Fizz had begun to appear at restaurant brunches and in suburban settings around the country. When the *Dallas Morning News* called for a return to "Those Glory Drinks of Yesteryear" in 1983, one of its examples was "that old favorite that's enjoying a new renaissance, the Ramos Fizz."

Many received the drink as a California export, downplaying or ignoring its New Orleans provenance. It was a specialty of the house at the San Francisco Bar and Grill in Tucson, the Bull Ring in Santa Fe offered a "California version of a Ramos gin fizz," and you could even find a Ramos Fizz brunch at the Old San Francisco restaurant in Sydney, Australia. In the late 1970s a half-dozen papers around the country printed the recipe for a "Golden State Ramos Fizz" (see page 120), which the *Chicago Tribune* (1979) said "brightens cold winter weekends [with] a sunny California feeling." Although the *Las Vegas Review-Journal* (1976) did note that the drink was "a favorite in New Orleans, too," a

Canadian newspaper (*Regina Leader-Post,* 1979) said the Ramos Fizz was "peculiar to San Francisco" and passed on a recipe featuring orange liqueur and sliced strawberries brought back from there by a reader.

But fashion is famously fickle. The Ramos Fizz fad faded even faster than it had appeared. More than four times as many California restaurants advertised their Ramos Fizzes in the single decade of the 1980s as in the next thirty years. These days Sam's Anchor Café in Tiburon still offers "Sam's Famous Ramos," but something called Sam's Smoothie is more popular.

## THE CLASSIC COCKTAIL RENAISSANCE

It's ironic that California's love affair with the Ramos Fizz cooled down just as *Food Arts* magazine observed in 1991 that "Bartenders from coast to coast have noticed a return to classic cocktails." As an example, the article mentioned the Ramos Gin Fizz. What was going on?

To review: The Ramos Fizz flourished for its first thirty years, crashed with Prohibition, rose again for the next thirty years, then languished as a bar drink for another thirty (while maintaining a strange half-life as a brunch libation in restaurants and homes in California and elsewhere), which brings us to the early 1990s. Time to rise again. In *Straight Up or On the Rocks* (1995), William Grimes, deploring "abominations like the Jell-O shot," pointed out that the Sazerac and Ramos Gin Fizz "are solid classics [that] await rediscovery." And that's what happened.

Just as Baby Boomers had rejected their parents' Martinis and Old-Fashioneds, Gen X bartenders scorned the Boomers' Slippery Nipples and Long Island Iced Tea. They revived classics from pre-Prohibition bar books, used fresh juices and sought out obscure brands, even made their own bitters—and charged double-digit prices. The result was worth all the tattoos, suspenders, and vintage facial hair. All "craft" bartenders knew how to make a Ramos Fizz.

As classic cocktails became fashionable once again, home bartenders began to mix them, too. The Ramos Fizz shared fully in this revival. Each year since 2015 *Difford's*

Ramos Gin Fizz candle. Courtesy of Jasmine Agosti, Swizzle Candles.

*Guide* has listed the most-viewed of more than twenty thousand cocktail recipes on its website, and the Ramos has been consistently in the top forty. (It peaked at number seven in the stay-at-home year 2022.)

This comeback means that once again association with the Ramos can be used to sell other things. The Holy Black Trading Company sells Ramos Gin Fizz soap, for instance, with a scent "all creamsicle and a barely detectible hint of juniper." A Charleston, South Carolina, firm offers a hand-poured Ramos Gin Fizz candle, that "captures the essence of the iconic drink with its blend of gin, cream, and lemon scents." An Austin brewery honors Ramos's first saloon with Imperial Cabinet wild ale, one in Philadelphia makes a Ramos Gin Fizz Milkshake IPA, and RVK Brewing Company of Reykjavik, Iceland, once offered a Ramos Gin Fizz Sour Ale (although it seems to have been discontinued).

The renewed appreciation for the Ramos Fizz since the turn of the twenty-first century also began to challenge an unfortunate tendency, beginning in the 1950s, to see the Ramos as a drink only for breakfast or brunch—like the Bloody Mary and the Mimosa. This prejudice is still widespread: In *Gin: A Global History* (2012) it's called "a traditional morning to midday tipple," for instance, and AFew Cocktails.com (2021) says it is "an elegant drink generally reserved for an early morning breakfast or brunch." In New Orleans, of course, many restaurants and bars have always been happy to shake up a Ramos for tourists any time of the day or night, but even there, DrunkardsAlmanac.com observes, it is "generally considered a brunch or day drink, so you can still have a Sazerac or two in the evening." The first of the "Tips for Drinking in New Orleans" in Sarah Baird's *New Orleans Cocktails* (2017) is, "The Ramos Gin Fizz is a brunch drink." Baird sees ordering one after brunch hours as a faux pas, "like asking for Eggs Benedict at 8 p.m." But many craft bartenders recognize, as Carl Ramos's customers did, that the Ramos Fizz makes a fine sundowner, aperitif, or even nightcap.

The renaissance also means that it's easier than ever before to find a Ramos Fizz outside New Orleans. These days all of the nation's twenty-five largest cities have at least one bar that serves a Ramos (and I stopped checking after twenty-five). It's also not that hard to find one outside the United States. The return to the classics was initially a phenomenon of the big cities of the American North and West, but it soon went international, and took the Ramos Fizz with it. The American Bar at London's Savoy Hotel was mixing Ramos Fizzes in Prohibition days; now a half-dozen hot new places in England do, too, including one in Birmingham that offers a prebatched "Hand Pull" Ramos

Rock musician Jim Morrison's friend Frank Lisciandro recalled waking up one morning in 1969 with a terrible hangover:

> [Jim] called over the waiter and ordered us each a Ramos Gin Fizz. "You'll feel a lot better after a couple of these," he promised, "and later you'll be able to eat lunch."
>
> The Ramos was cold and delicious and I felt less sick after absorbing a tall one. . . . The second Ramos Gin Fizz got my blood surging and my headache mysteriously disappeared.

In the 1991 movie *The Doors,* a hungover Morrison, played by Val Kilmer, looks warily at a plate of eggs: "Ugh, I can't eat this stuff, it'll really make me sick. Gimme a Dos Equis, will ya Delores? And a Ramos gin fizz with it."

---

Fizz from an ale pump. An afternoon on the internet also found the drink at places in Dublin, Paris, Copenhagen, and Nitra, Slovakia. There were another half-dozen in Australia, including one in Sydney that claims to serve "hundreds of these cocktails every week," and Asia boasted a dozen or so—Bali and Bangalore, Saigon and Singapore,

Taipei and Seoul, Phuket. . . . Not all of these places mix according to Ramos. One serves its Fizz over ice, another omits the egg white, others include Cointreau, Chartreuse, or coconut milk. But they're trying.

## BUT KEEP IN MIND . . .

The Ramos's twenty-first-century comeback has been impressive, to be sure, but it has been partial. No one thinks now that drinking one is a required experience for visitors to New Orleans. It seems unlikely that journalists will ever again be able to assume that their readers will recognize an allusion to it, or that it will become a staple of middle-class entertaining, as it did in 1970s California. In truth, its renewed renown has been pretty much limited to craft bars and cocktail geeks. Moreover, even in those circles its ubiquity may not last. Now that the classic cocktail revolution has succeeded, what next? There have been foreshadowings of a disco drink revival, "elevating" the reviled fern bar drinks of the 1970s and 1980s. Could the

Ramos be shouldered aside by an artisanal Teeny Weeny Woo Woo? On the other hand, some predict a return to simpler drinks, with fewer ingredients, but that would also pretty much rule out a fussy drink like the Ramos. And what about a writer who deprecates cocktail "nostalgia" and calls for a "terroir-minded" approach "in which people and place supercede devotion to the classics"? I don't think he means that the Ramos Fizz shouldn't be on bar menus outside New Orleans, but then again, he might.

In years to come, if you want a Ramos Fizz, you may have to mix one yourself. There are lots of recipes on the internet, but many are lame, or weird. In "150 Sensational Recipes to Make in Your Blender," for instance, *Good Housekeeping* omits the egg white; the 1988 *Mr. Boston Official Bartender's Guide* substitutes triple sec for orange flower water and serves the drink with two ice cubes.

So you'd better read the chapter starting on page 75.

CHAPTER FOUR

# Historical Interlude

## THE KINGFISH SCHOOLS SOME YANKEES

As governor of Louisiana from 1928 until 1932, Huey "Kingfish" Long evoked strong feelings. His supporters, not without reason, saw him as a champion of the common man, providing good roads and free textbooks, standing up against the oil companies and the rich. His enemies, also with reason, saw him as an American Mussolini, dealing ruthlessly with opposition and not particularly concerned with legality. Everyone agreed, however, that he had an extraordinary gift for self-promotion.

And he loved his Ramos Fizz. It's said that when he traveled out of state, he sometimes took along a bartender named Henri so he could have ones like he had back home, and people joked that he liked the ones at the Sazerac Bar in New Orleans so much so that he had the Airline Highway built so he could get there from Baton Rouge forty minutes faster. When he moved on from the governorship to the U.S. Senate, a wire service profile included his recipe (see page 119), which—note well—called for six drops of vanilla extract.

July 25, 1935, was a great day in Ramos history. As the *New York Times* reported, at the Hotel New Yorker in Manhattan, Long "staged a one-man circus in the circular bar on the main floor demonstrating to newspapermen, photographers, waiters, bartenders and hotel guests how to make the celebrated New Orleans Ramos gin fizz." He explained to the crowd: "Well, gentlemen, I stopped in here at the bar yesterday. I have been . . . on the water wagon for 18 months and wouldn't think of going off. Well, I saw a sign 'Ramos Gin Fizz.' Wondering if one could get the real thing here, I ordered one. Gentlemen, it was terrible. The second one tasted more terrible and the third one tasted most terrible. I dashed off a telegram to Sam here to take

Hotel New Yorker claims to serve a Ramos Gin Fizz. Advertisement in the *New York Times,* 1935.

> It looks like the stuff they spread on airfields for a plane coming in for a crash landing.
>
> —STAN DELAPLANE, *San Francisco Chronicle* (1972)

the first plane up." He introduced Sam Guarino, head bartender at the Roosevelt Hotel, who had flown in from New Orleans that morning: "Now this here chap knows how to make a Ramos gin fizz." He continued, "The Ramos fizz is native to Louisiana. My grandpappy introduced it back in 1852. We saved the Ramos fizz for the American people during Prohibition. I'm performing a public service showing you how."

Long "assisted" with the mixing and distribution, posing for photographers with shaker in hand. Repeating that he was "on the water wagon," he said, "I'm merely sampling this to make sure you gentlemen are getting the real thing." He continued sampling. Raising what was, by one reporter's count, his fifth glass, he said, "And this is, gentlemen, my gift to New York."

Huey Long and Sam Guarino on the cover of *Business Week.* Courtesy of Bloomberg Businessweek.

After that, the *Times* reported, "the Kingfish left the bar with a broad grin, leading a crowd of reporters to his apartment on the 22nd floor of the hotel, where he spent two hours discoursing on the political situation."

Long was plainly positioning himself to run for president on a radical "Share the Wealth" platform, so it's not surprising that his antics made nationwide news. Long and Guarino appeared on the cover of *Business Week,* and the *Fort Worth Star-Telegram* remarked, "Thirty seven years elapsed between the sinking of the Maine and Huey Long's illustrated lecture in New York on the mixing of Ramos gin fizz. . . . Both events will be shown in newsreel form at the Palace Theater tomorrow." The *Kansas City Star* added, "While the 'Share the Wealth' patriarch may be a pain in the neck to you, see his photoplay bit and you will have to admit he is a showman."

The story lingered in the news for days, with one twist after another. The first came when a wire service story reported, "Bartenders below the Mason-Dixon line are throwing up their hands in horror at the mere thought of vanilla in a gin fizz," and wondered if Long had "committed political suicide" by including it. The United Press reported that "dispatches from New Orleans reflected the greatest indignation," adding that "some of the Kingfish's many enemies there said he knew nothing about refined drinks." The *Chattanooga Daily Times* observed, "Men have been shot for less than he has done. [He] would be wise to be less blatant on the subject of the composition of that mystic drink—a question which has started feuds, divided families, almost caused civil warfare to break out among the connoisseurs in the pleasant Creole city." The crosstown *Chattanooga News* editorialized, "Huey Long put vanilla in his alleged Ramos fizz. That shows us what the man is like." The controversy got a boost when Sam Guarino himself declared that the drink should not include vanilla. Although papers announced that Guarino had "turned on his patron," Long may well have encouraged him as a way to keep the story in the news. Long went on WHN radio and denied that he had advocated substituting vanilla for orange flower water—which wasn't what he had been accused of—and claimed that reporters who said he had were drunk.

As the vanilla hullabaloo died down, Long's older brother Julius provoked another burst of stories when he announced that "John M. Long, our grandfather, was a farmer and never saw nor made a Ramos gin fizz." He said that if Huey was going to make up stories about his relatives, "he might as well claim credit for some great things, such as winning the battle of New Orleans or the Mexican war." Long replied, "After all these years, if it develops that I have been wrong and that my grandfather never did have a Ramos gin fizz, then he was woefully mistreated. And that being the case, the present living members of the family are entitled to more than their regular share."

Meanwhile, bartenders across the country reported increased demand for the drink. King's Restaurant in Fitchburg, Massachusetts, and Al's Tavern in New Brunswick, New Jersey, advertised their versions of "Huey Long's Ramos Gin Fizz"; and Sam Guarino was booked for guest appearances at bars in Cincinnati, Louisville, Detroit, and Minneapolis. In his column for the *New York Sun,* H. I. Phillips wrote that Huey's demonstration had been one of "the banner events of the summer," along with King George's jubilee.

Why did this story get such a ridiculous amount of attention? The *Brooklyn Citizen* suggested a reason: the Kingfish "contributed enormously to the gayety [*sic*] of the people during the doleful depression," with his "bizarre and agile imagination" and ability to "talk for hours without saying anything, all the while keeping the galleries roaring with laughter." Only a month earlier he had staged a fifteen-hour filibuster in the Senate, enlivened by his recipes for pot likker and fried oysters.

The laughter stopped on September 10, when Long was assassinated in Baton Rouge, but a decade later, in *The Stork Club Bar Book* (1946), journalist and bon vivant Lucius Beebe wrote of Huey at the New Yorker: "Though there were those present who might condemn his brand of politics, there was no one who would even implicitly reproach either his virtuosity as a barkeep or his capacity as his own best customer."

CHAPTER FIVE

# Ingredients

The Ramos Fizz wasn't created ex nihilo. There are several ways Ramos could have tweaked or combined existing drinks. In 1885, while still in Baton Rouge, he was already known for mixing dairy and citrus in "his choice milk lemonades." He would also have known a drink called a Silver Fizz: take one of those, add some lime juice, a splash of cream, and a few drops of orange flower water, shake well, and you have the drink that now carries his name. It may sound simple, but others' attempted imitations were unsuccessful. Ti Martin of Commander's Palace told *Garden & Gun* magazine in 2021, "I can't think of anything else quite like its masterful combination of ingredients and technique."

## THE ORIGINAL RECIPE

The Montana visitor I quoted earlier wrote in 1911, "There are thousands amongst the thirst-crazed multitude in this fair city who have grown prematurely gray worrying that Ramos might die and his secret die with him." For a while it looked as if that might happen. As Prohibition approached, Ramos himself said he was going to burn the recipe and take its secrets to his grave. But he finally shared it with a reporter for the *New Orleans Item-Tribune* in 1925. Here it is, as printed:

One and Only One

RAMOS ORIGINAL GIN FIZZ

One tablespoon powdered sugar.

Three or four drops of Orange Flower Water.

One-half Lime (Juice).

One-half Lemon (Juice).

One Jigger of Old Tom Gin.

(Old Gordon may be used but a sweet gin is preferable.)

The white of one egg.

One-half glass of crushed ice.

About 2 tablespoonsful of rich milk or cream.

A little Seltzer water (about an ounce) to make it pungent.

Together well shaken and strained. (drink freely)

In 2007 David Wondrich observed in his column for *Esquire* that each ingredient is essential: "The egg white gives it body, the cream lends smoothness, and the citrus provides its cool. The sugar tames the citrus, the gin does what gin does, and the seltzer wakes the whole thing up. As for the orange flower water—that's for mystery." Let's look at those ingredients one at a time.

## SUGAR

This is a refined drink, which calls for refined—that is, white—sugar. Save that Demerara for Old-Fashioneds. And do use Louisiana's own cane sugar.

Note that when Ramos called for powdered sugar, he did not mean what we call "powdered sugar" today. That commercial compound, also called "confectioner's sugar," includes an anticaking agent like cornstarch. Ramos meant what Sam Guarino of the old Roosevelt Hotel called "pulverized sugar"—sugar ground to a powder. You can pulverize your own by throwing some in a blender or spice grinder.

### ORANGE FLOWER WATER

Some recipes substitute orange bitters, orange liqueur, or even just orange juice, but accept no substitute. In *The Essential Cocktail* (2010), acclaimed cocktail expert Dale DeGroff says, "if you can't find orange-flower water, put off making this fizz until you can." Orange flower water is made by boiling blossoms of the bitter orange tree in water and condensing the fragrant steam. It is widely used in Mediterranean and Middle Eastern cookery, and these days it is easily procured online, but different brands vary widely in strength and quality. Portland bartender Jeffrey

Morgenthaler has made a study of it and on his website recommends the French brand Theodule Noirot.

### LEMON AND LIME

You need both. They're complementary, with different acidity, and lime has a bitter note that lemon lacks. Ramos probably used small lemons, with about the same amount of juice as limes, so one tablespoon of each kind of juice is about right. I've seen recipes that call for bottled ReaLemon, Rose's Lime Juice, frozen lemonade and/or limeade concentrate, sour mix . . . They're all abominations. Squeeze your own lemons and limes, and try to do it no more than a few hours before you need them.

### OLD TOM GIN

Old Tom was what Mark Vierthaler calls "the go-to spirit of the titans of classic mixology," and Chris McMillian has found that Ramos used the popular Burnett's brand. Compared to today's popular London dry gins, Old Toms were sweeter and less "botanical"—meaning primarily that the juniper presence was less assertive. (Some were barrel-aged, which made for a richer taste, but if the Burnett brand was one of them, the label didn't mention it.)

Ramos's brand [*left*] and a twenty-first-century tribute. From Dixie Pix.

Although Old Tom virtually disappeared in the twentieth century, the cocktail revival prompted many distillers to bring their versions to market, and now it's easy to find the real thing. The Sazerac Company, for instance, now markets Henry Ramos Gin, Old Tom–style and 85.6 proof, "in honor of Henry Ramos's birth year of 1856." As for quantity, at the time a "jigger" was a stemmed sherry glass that held a little more than one ounce.

### EGG WHITE

Eggs are bigger now than they were in Ramos's day, so use the white of a medium egg, or use the white of a large one and discard a teaspoonful. (Salmonella? See below.)

### CRUSHED ICE

You want just enough to chill the drink without diluting it more than necessary, and you don't need to be precise. Ramos was probably using ice chipped with an ice pick off a big block. You don't really need to crush it either, as long as it melts while you shake. In vintage recipes, "one-half glass" could be either one ounce or two. One doesn't sound like enough, so aim for about a quarter cup of ice. A couple of cubes will probably do it.

---

In Walker Percy's novel *Love in the Ruins,* Dr. Thomas More says, "I begin to drink Ramos gin fizzes with one swallow. At one time I was allergic to egg whites but that was long ago. These drinks feel silky and benign." That is, until he breaks out in hives and his throat closes up.

Percy was drawing on personal experience. He himself once went into anaphylactic shock while drinking Ramoses. In his 1975 essay "Bourbon," he wrote, "Anybody who monkeys around with gin and egg white deserves what he gets. I should have stuck with Bourbon and have from that day to this."

---

### RICH MILK OR CREAM

Half-and-half could work as "rich milk," but why not go whole-hog with 100 percent heavy cream? As the late San Francisco bartender Adam Richey said, if you care about calories, drink vodka and soda. Just for the record, by the way, I've encountered a recipe calling for Greek yogurt instead of cream, and another suggesting vanilla ice cream.

## SELTZER WATER

Seltzer is just plain water carbonated with carbon dioxide. Most likely, Ramos used a soda siphon called a gasogene to produce it. If all you can get is club soda, don't worry about it. It has various minerals added, but it's hard to tell the difference.

## GARNISHES

In general, less is more. Ramos didn't garnish his Fizz. Now you do see cherries, orange wedges, sprigs of mint, sprinklings of nutmeg, saffron, all kinds of clutter—but, personally, I think its pristine white magnificence should be savored with minimal distraction.

To make a Ramos Fizz like the original, see the recipe on page 111, but read this first:

> The Ramos Gin Fizz persists for the same reason that chefs still bake soufflés, or engineers still hand-assemble Ferraris, or that directors kept casting Marlon Brando. Yes, it is notoriously difficult work, but you can't deny the finished product's greatness.
>
> —JASON O'BRYAN, *Robb Report* (2021)

### THE VANILLA QUESTION

In 1937 Stanley Clisby Arthur wrote, "Veteran barkeepers differ violently—practically come to blows—over the inclusion of . . . two innocent drops of extract of vanilla" in the Ramos. Ramos didn't call for it, but some serious people think it may have been an undisclosed secret ingredient. To settle the question, Arthur suggested that one take it up with Paul Alpuente at the Hotel Roosevelt, who had been Ramos's partner and head bartender at the Stag Saloon. "When he mixes your Ramos gin fizz, watch him closely." (When the *Detroit Free Press* printed a recipe attributed to Alpuente some years later, it had no vanilla.)

Even if vanilla wasn't in Ramos's original Fizz, though,

many think it's a good addition. In *The Waldorf Astoria Bar Book,* Frank Caiafa says that "some of New Orleans' finer establishments" add a touch of it and modern recipes frequently call for one to three drops or at least list it as optional.

Here's a thought. In Ramos's day, Old Tom gins that were aged in oak barrels picked up a touch of vanilla flavor and aroma. Ramos's favored Burnett brand may or may not have been one of them, but there's a rationale for adding a drop or two of vanilla. (Imitation extract is fine; in fact, it's often made with vanillin from American oak.)

## AN ASIDE ON SALMONELLA

There is raw egg in homemade mayonnaise, cookie dough, hollandaise and bearnaise sauces, chocolate mousse, tiramisu, and, yes, in a Ramos Fizz. And it's true that eating raw eggs can expose you to a nasty bug called salmonella. But eating steak tartare or sushi can, too, so why do eggs get such a bad rap?

I'm not going to suggest that you just ignore the risk, but you might think about the numbers. The CDC estimates that one in every twenty thousand eggs carries salmonella. So if you drink, say, two Ramoses a week, every week, you can expect to run into a contaminated egg every 190 years or so. Of course, drinking two a day is another matter.

Anyway, if you get salmonellosis, it's quite possible that you won't know it and very unlikely that you'll need medical attention. If you do show symptoms, they will be really unpleasant, but they'll almost always clear up within a few days. In short, adopting the stereotypical New Orleans devil-may-care attitude is unlikely to put you in mortal danger.

But if your immune system is compromised—or if you're just the type of person who wears an N95 mask when driving alone—you can buy pasteurized egg whites in cartons at the grocery store. Pasteurization makes it harder to whip the whites, so your foam might suffer, but shaking the whites for a minute or two before adding the citrus juice will help. Audrey Saunders of Pegu Club thinks pasteurized eggs add a "really funky wet-diaper nose," but there's not much to be done about that.

Raw or pasteurized, keep your eggs chilled until you're ready to use them. If you can't do that, make some other drink. (Don't even *think* about using powdered egg whites.)

> I went back to the hotel, and watched eagerly while the old barman put little dashes of this and that together and then handed it all to the strong young stevedore who was chief shaker. I decided that infinite care, unhurried patience, and a never varying formula were more the secret than any magic element such as dried nectar-crumbs or drops from a Ramos philter.
>
> —M. F. K. FISHER, *Consider the Oyster* (1988)

## THE MODERN RAMOS

The ingredients of today's Ramos Gin Fizz are pretty much what they were at the Imperial Cabinet, but there have been a few minor changes. Most recipes today use simple syrup (equal parts sugar and water) in place of powdered sugar, and they're likely to be sweeter. Most call for London dry gin instead of Old Tom, the white of a large egg rather than a medium one, and a standard 1½- or 2-ounce jigger. Some call for vanilla or allow it as an option. Ramos stipulated three or four drops of orange flower water, but these days there's no consensus about that. One recipe calls for a single drop, added after the drink is poured, simply for aroma; another calls for eight to ten drops. Tastes differ. Moreover, how much to use depends partly on the brand, since they differ in strength. Be careful, though: too much and (as one critic put it) it smells like "old lady perfume."

See page 113 for a Ramos that sort of averages the amounts of ingredients called for by modern recipes.

CHAPTER SIX

# Techniques

Amy C. Collins observes that Carl Ramos's "namesake classic is notoriously loathed by bartenders"—not as a drink, but as an order.

> A well-made Ramos is a real treat, but it basically requires a whole chemistry experiment to bring its many ingredients together.
>
> —*HUFFINGTON POST,* "Bartenders Reveal the Drinks They'd Never Order Themselves" (2023)

## WHAT BARTENDERS HAVE TO SAY

They don't hold back:

Jeffrey Morgenthaler: "the scourge of day bartenders everywhere, . . . easily one of the most complicated drinks in history."

St. John Frizell: "messy, it's really messy, hard to keep together, . . . just really annoying."

Mark Schettler: "the most aggravating cocktail in the history of bartending."

Sarah Baird: "the most physically exhausting cocktail made on the regular behind modern bars today."

Mauro Villalobos: "If you have proper bar etiquette in a busy bar, don't order this, or order it if you hate the bartender."

Aaron Pringle: "such a gargantuan pain in the ass you kinda just want to pretend it never existed."

Frankie Hung (Taiwan): "hàochēng tiáo jiǔ shī mèngyǎn de [a bartender's nightmare]."

Derek Andros: "Most bartenders would give you $2 and ask you to order it across the street."

Jason O'Bryan: "far and away the most difficult cocktail to make. . . . There would be very little reason to make it ever if it wasn't so, so, so, so good."

## SHAKE IT UP, BABY

Yes, bartenders often sigh when someone orders a Ramos Fizz. There's that complicated list of ingredients, of course, but mostly it's what one London bar explicitly lists as another: elbow grease. *The Gourmet's Guide to New Orleans Creole Cookbook* (1933) insists that "the real art in making a Gin Fizz is in proper shaking. Don't just shake it up a few times and think you have done the job, because it is only started." Carl Ramos himself said, "Be sure to use an airtight shaker and to shake and shake and shake until there is not a bubble left."

Naturally, many people have turned to various devices to avoid all this work—milkshake spindles, stand or immersion blenders, nitrous oxide cream whippers, something called an ultrasonic homogenizer . . . These gizmos can give you a drink that tastes really good, but it will have the uniform consistency of a milkshake. That's not necessarily a bad thing, but it is a *different* thing. I won't go as far as Chloe Frechette, who says that "lacking its characteristic frothy head [the Ramos] appears floppy, flaccid, and sad," but traditionalists do think that a real Fizz, the classic, should be shaken.

Shaker boys are hard to find these days, but with enough ingenuity or cash you can find a shaking machine. As early as the 1890s, bartenders were messing around with something called a Cole shaker, a hand-cranked device with two glass cylinders originally used for milkshakes, and there have been many variations since. By far the coolest is the hand-cranked Imperial MK2 Champion Shaker, invented by Jason Crawley (upward of four grand, plus shipment from Australia). Its cast iron and brass give it a great steampunk look, and Neiman Marcus even sold a five-foot-tall model for home use (thirty-five thousand dollars, with four cases of Tanqueray thrown in). If you adapt a motorized Taiwanese bubble tea shaker, you don't even have to crank. You want to shake for six minutes? Twelve? No problem.

But why? Maybe a bartender who's turning out Ramoses day after day can be excused for seeking shortcuts, but those of us mixing drinks at home for friends and family should probably stick to the old-fashioned method. The *Birmingham News* said that at the Stag Saloon "this process of shaking the silver mug was hardly less than a ceremonial." You can bring some of that ceremony to your house. It's not *that* much work, and it links you to a long and honorable tradition. (If you insist on technology, maybe sneak a wire mixing ball into your shaker, the kind used to blend protein shakes.)

How long to shake? Well, there certainly was a whole lot of shaking going on in the old days, but there's been some exaggeration in the telling. By 1921, two years into

Imperial MK2 Champion Shaker. Courtesy of Jason Crawley.

Prohibition, the *Item* newspaper was recalling that the drink was shaken for ten minutes, now you may hear twelve or even twenty, but an 1895 newspaper story said that two minutes was standard at the Imperial Cabinet. In

1908 the *Kansas City Star* said it took five minutes at the Stag, but given that the shaker boys had become a tourist attraction, some of that increase may have been for show. When Sam Guarino was showing New Yorkers how to make a Ramos, he said to shake for two and a half to three minutes (although on another occasion he said five minutes, "no more, no less"). Ramos himself told a reporter in 1926 to shake for, "oh, say two or three minutes—until the mixture has a creamy, fluffy, silvery consistency, with no bubbles showing."

So you don't have to go full Jerry Lee on this. Five minutes is plenty, and three is probably enough. In fact, a couple of recipes say "shake vigorously fifty times," which takes me about thirty seconds, and famous New Orleans bartender Chris Hannah, who used to say at least two minutes was required, now says twenty-five to forty-five seconds is enough. I'm not going to argue with the 2022 Bartender of the Year, but I'll stick with three to five minutes. Can't hurt.

There are some variations on the basic shake you might consider. In the mid-aughts, for instance, a technique was revived that had been around, unused, since the 1950s:

what's called a "dry shake"—first without ice, then with—yielding a frothier drink. Here again, though, there's no consensus on how long to shake. Hannah says ten seconds without ice and a vigorous fifteen seconds with ice gives a perfect result, but his renowned crosstown compeer Chris McMillian plumps for a minute or two without ice and at least a minute with.

Then there are those who argue for a "reverse dry shake"—first with ice, then without (usually adding the egg white for the second part only). One advantage is that you don't lose foam by straining out the ice when you pour the drink in the glass. That's also true for another method: shake just once with two ice cubes in the shaker until they're completely melted and you don't hear them anymore. This limits dilution and means you don't need to keep an eye on the clock.

---

In New Orleans at Easter, Chris Hannah at the Jewel of the South serves Easter egg–colored Ramos Fizzes.

---

But however you shake the drink, you need to address the question of when to add the seltzer. Ramos put it in before shaking, and doing that, or adding it for the second half of a dry or reverse-dry shake, makes for a good, conservative result. However, most bartenders these days layer some in the glass before pouring the drink, add it gingerly to top up, or both. If you want the towering head that has become the Ramos's signature, let the glass rest in the freezer for a few minutes, then top up, *slowly.*

## FOAM INFLATION

About that towering head, though: Carl Ramos never saw one.

When the Ramos Fizz made an appearance in the 1947 movie *Dead Reckoning,* one old-timer complained to the *Cincinnati Enquirer* that the drink on the screen bore no resemblance to what he remembered drinking before Prohibition: the glass was too big and the liquid too "fuzzy." It seems that as late as the 1930s the drink was usually served in something like a juice glass. The one at the Roosevelt Hotel's Sazerac Bar, for instance, was originally four and a half inches high and held only about six and a half ounces. This implies that at the time a big foamy head wasn't seen as important, and indeed Carl Ramos's instructions for shaking didn't produce one—just as well, because if you do the numbers on his recipe, a six-and-a-half-ounce glass is barely large enough without any head at all. An eight-ounce glass makes for a more comfortable fit. The Sazerac Bar eventually adopted that size, and it became more or less the standard for a while. The recipe in the 1938 *New*

Then and now. From Dixie Pix.

*Orleans City Guide* calls for an eight-ounce glass, and many recipes still do.

But different shaking techniques and topping off with soda water can produce what cocktail writer Jane Ryan has described as an "exquisitely frothy cap that rises above the glass like a boozy Pixar-animated cloud." This requires an even bigger glass: Riedel Crystal's "Drink Specific Fizz Glass" is a tall, slim number that holds a bit more than nine ounces, and many recipes these days call for an even larger Collins glass.

The search for that massive head of foam set off something of an arms race in the early years of the cocktail revival. YouTube is awash with videos of bartenders (many from Taiwan, for some reason) coaxing the last millimeter of foam from their Fizzes before the whole thing topples. As Oklahoma City bartender Charles Friedrichs says, "At the end of the day, the bartender with the biggest head claims bragging rights!"

Boys think size matters, of course—which makes it amusing that a woman may have retired the title. At Death & Co in Los Angeles, Devon Tarby brought a nitrous oxide cream whipper to the foam fight. Starting with the regular single-serving ingredients, she produced a supersized Ramos that rose a full two inches above the rim of an enormous eighteen-ounce glass.

Chris McMillian thinks this has gotten out of hand. He says, "The drink is now judged on how high of a meringue there is, but that's a parlor trick." He calls for a return to the Roosevelt Hotel six-ounce glass. "The drink cannot taste as designed if not served in that glass." Contrarian barkeep Giuseppe González concurs. He sniffs that the latter-day version isn't a Ramos at all, just "a pretty Tom Collins topped with meringue."

---

Two Harvard physicists walk into a bar . . .

The *Boston Globe* was there in 2012 when they ordered a Ramos Gin Fizz—

> The scientists spoke of surfactants and nucleating bubbles as [the bartender] poured the drink into a tall glass. When he reached the rim, he kept going, creating a tower of fizzy foam. Just as the scientists had said, the liquid ingredients had been transformed into a solid made of liquid and air—a stiff foam that held up a metal straw.

---

CHAPTER SEVEN

# Riffs, Spins, Takes, Twists, Plays, Etc.

The many variations on the classic Ramos Fizz over the years illustrate bartender Phil Ward's "Mr. Potato Head" theory of cocktail innovation: simply swapping out one or more ingredients of an existing recipe can create something quite different. The drink's nine ingredients can all be messed with, singly or in combination, and you can always add one or two more, so recent years have seen scores of riffs on Carl Ramos's original. At some point you have to ask how much you can change it and have it remain recognizably a riff on the Ramos, but a look around suggests that just about any drink with citrus, cream, and egg white qualifies.

## DEPARTURES FROM THE ORIGINAL

As early as 1910 a bartender at the Baltimore Country Club was adding a teaspoonful of maraschino to his otherwise orthodox New Orleans Fizz. That same year a manual of mixed drinks included a "New Orleans Fiss" that called for a violet liqueur called Crême Yvette instead of orange flower water. About the same time the Blackstone Hotel in Chicago replaced the orange flower water with grenadine in their "Remus Fizz." Other early recipes replaced or supplemented orange flower water with orange bitters, orgeat, or kirsch, and an Argentine bar manual called for adding "*un chorro de Chartreuse.*"

But these pre–World War II riffs were nothing compared to what has been seen in the craft cocktail era. (Google tells us that in 2017 the word "riff" was five and a half times more common in American English than it had been thirty years earlier.) As before, many variations simply involve substitutions for orange flower water, among them triple sec, frozen orange juice concentrate, and bitter orange marmalade. Other recipes leave the orange family altogether and turn to substitutes like rose water and cardamom tincture. One of the strangest is made by infusing pure grain alcohol with yellow sheet cake.

Innovators have also essayed a bewildering variety of additions—absinthe, garlic, and Jägermeister, just for starters. Gin has been replaced by everything from Tequila to Talisker, Campari to Calvados. Fizz has come from prosecco, kombucha, and fruity energy drink. Cream has been replaced by Fruit Loop milk punch. Notable two-ingredient switcheroos involve whiskey for gin and beer for seltzer; white rum for gin and green Chartreuse for orange flower water; peaty Scotch for gin with violet liqueur for simple syrup. (The first two won competitions for beer and rum cocktails, respectively.)

The twenty-first century has seen a tribute to the national drink of Argentina in the form of a Fizz made with

Fernet Branca and Coca-Cola (see page 127), as well as several attempts at a Ramos Fizz–Piña Colada hybrid. There's a Japanese take with squid ink, garnished with nori (dried seaweed), and a Lebanese version with Za'atar-infused gin and jallab (date molasses and rose water). There's a Carrot Cake Ramos Fizz with heirloom carrot juice and cinnamon syrup.

In the farther reaches of molecular mixology, Singapore's Aki Eguchi uses agar agar, xanthan gum, and modified soy protein to produce a clarified Crystal Ramos Gin Fizz garnished with orange blossom bubbles, and Eben Freeman in New York has created a chewy Ramos Gin Fizz Marshmallow, tossed in juniper sugar.

I will note reluctantly that there are vegan versions of the Ramos Fizz (see page 124), and, if you insist, you can even make one alcohol-free. One recipe calls for replacing the gin with chamomile or mint tea, or you could use one of the many nonalcoholic "gins" on the market, but even better might be just to leave the gin out. A couple of California bars did that once (see page 122) and apparently nobody noticed.

Clarified Ramos Gin Fizz in Singapore. Courtesy of Jigger & Pony Group, Singapore.

> Looks like a frothy glass of milk and smells slightly like aftershave. . . . a taste of history and pretty damn fine at that.
> —CHRISTOPHER HIRST in the *Independent,* London (2005)

## A CURMUDGEONLY VIEW

If you think you've detected an occasional note of disapproval in this discussion, you're not mistaken. I guess mixologists gotta mix, but in my opinion, it's hard to improve on what *Texas Monthly* (2015) calls "the Cadillac of Cocktails." Moreover, some find the competitive, show-off aspect of this zealous search for innovation alien to the spirit of the drink. David Wondrich is one of them. "It's a subtle drink," he says. "And everyone who has added stuff to it is trying to get it to punch above its weight, and that's misguided to me. It's supposed to be a cloud you lay back on, sit back and float a while. It's not some mano-a-mano experience. Make something different if you want to do that."

There's also the matter of tradition. A riff on a classic can be seen as harmless amusement or even a tribute, but it can also verge on disrespect. In 2022 New Orleans saloonkeeper Neal Bodenheimer told *Southern Kitchen,* "There are things here that are sacred to us locally, and there are things we can play around with. What people get wrong about interpreting New Orleans drinks is they take things, like the Ramos Gin Fizz, that we hold pretty near and dear, that we don't view as things we want to play with, and they play with them."

To be sure, one could say that the Ramos was itself a riff on the Silver Fizz, but somehow a riff that has been more popular than the original for such a long time is no longer a riff. Few variants of the Ramos Fizz have that potential.

But one thing no one has a problem with is working to *perfect* a classic. *Alcademics: The Study of Booze* reports that at the Tales of the Cocktail gathering in 2011 a team from Hendrick's Gin did for the Ramos what Austin's Aaron Franklin did for beef brisket: they made one with freshly laid eggs, cream from a cow milked on-site, and lemons picked from the tree. That's my kind of variation.

"You need a drink," he said with the air of a diagnostician.

"A drink," she answered bitterly. "I'm sick of the drinks we've been having. Gin, whiskey, rum, what else is there?"

He took her into a bar, and she cried, but he bought her a fancy mixed drink, something called a Ramos gin fizz, and she was a little appeased because she had never had one before.

—From MARY MCCARTHY, *The Company She Keeps* (1942)

Candor compels the admission that to absorb the native beverages of New Orleans it is most advantageous to be in New Orleans itself. Other atmospheres are vaguely hostile to the leisured formality and circumstance required both for the devising and appreciation of flips and fizzes.

—LUCIUS BEEBE, *The Stork Club Bar Book* (1946)

CHAPTER EIGHT

# Recipes

Some of these recipes are here just for historical interest or novelty value and aren't actually meant to be used. It should be obvious which those are.

Many of them call for "simple syrup." To make it, combine equal parts by volume of sugar and water in a saucepan over medium heat, stirring until the sugar has dissolved. Let the syrup cool completely before using it. It will keep for several weeks in the refrigerator.

For a better Fizz, have your cream and seltzer as cold as possible. Unless otherwise specified, use a Collins or similar glass, and chill it first.

# THE ORIGINAL RAMOS GIN FIZZ

This recipe will give you something like the pre-Prohibition drink served at the Imperial Cabinet (ca. 1890–1907) and the Stag (1907–1919). It's essentially the recipe Ramos gave out in 1925, with more precise measurements.

**1 tablespoon finely ground white sugar**

**3–4 drops orange flower water**

**1 tablespoon lime juice**

**1 tablespoon lemon juice**

**1¼ ounces Old Tom gin (see note below)**

**White of 1 medium egg (or white of 1 large egg less one teaspoon)**

**¼ cup crushed ice**

**2 tablespoons cream or half-and-half**

**2 tablespoons seltzer**

Put all ingredients in a shaker and shake for 3 minutes.

Strain the foamy result into a chilled 6½- to 8-ounce glass.

A sip will provide what one drinker called "a test of the senses," a drink "simultaneously creamy, silken, floral, rich, light, citrusy and frothy."

**NOTE:** If Old Tom is not available, go with a less junipery gin like Bombay Sapphire, New Amsterdam, or Fleischmann's, and increase the sugar in the recipe by ½ teaspoon.

## RAMOS'S SECRET SAUCE

Happy Golden, a Cincinnati vaudeville entertainer, had his first Ramos at the Imperial Cabinet, when he performed in New Orleans in 1904. Interviewed by the *Cincinnati Enquirer* in the 1940s, he recalled that the drink contained gin, egg white, cream, and "a dash of something which Ramos prepared in secret." Golden said that not even the bartenders knew what was in this "mysterious elixir"; when the bottles of it were empty, Ramos refilled them behind closed doors. Other visitors reported the same secrecy.

Working backward from the recipe Ramos made public, though, it's apparent that the elixir was basically an elevated sour mix, with fresh juices and a touch of orange flower water. Here's how to make enough for four drinks:

**¼ cup finely ground sugar**
**¼ cup freshly squeezed lime juice**
**¼ cup freshly squeezed lemon juice**
**12–16 drops orange flower water**

Combine juices and orange flower water.

Add sugar and shake or stir to dissolve.

Add 3 tablespoons of this to the gin, egg white, and cream the recipe calls for, then shake with the crushed ice and seltzer, and there you have it. Probably the bottled "Ramos Fizz Mix" advertised by a California supermarket in 1982 was something like this.

# A MODERN RAMOS GIN FIZZ

There has been some evolution since Ramos's time. This is a mashup of a dozen modern recipes from reputable sources, and it's a good way to start if you want to mix your own.

**2 ounces London dry or Old Tom gin**
**2 tablespoons 1:1 simple syrup (5 teaspoons if using Old Tom)**
**3–4 drops orange flower water**
**1 tablespoon lime juice**
**1 tablespoon lemon juice**
**White of 1 large egg**
**3 tablespoons heavy cream**
**2 ice cubes**
**2 tablespoons seltzer**
**2 drops vanilla (optional)**

Put all ingredients except cream, ice, and seltzer in a shaker and shake for three minutes.

Add cream and ice and shake for another minute or until you can't hear the ice anymore.

Strain into glass and put glass in the freezer for two or three minutes.

Top up *slowly* with seltzer.

# SHERRY FLIP

In its heyday Ramos's saloon was using hundreds of thousands of egg whites a year, so it stands to reason that he had hundreds of thousands of yolks left over. *Leslie's Weekly* reported that some were shipped to bakers all over the country to use for sponge cake, but others were scrambled for the saloon's free lunch, and many were used for Sherry Flips, which became a house specialty almost as well known locally as the Gin Fizz.

**Yolk of 1 egg**
**2 ounces dry sherry (ideally, oloroso)**
**½ teaspoon simple syrup, or to taste**
**Nutmeg, for garnish (optional)**

Shake egg yolk, sherry, and syrup with ice.
Strain into a small wineglass.
Grate nutmeg on top if desired.

# A CURE FOR THE KATZENJAMMERS

From Dixie Pix.

The Ramos Fizz is widely believed to be good for the morning after a night of excess. Frank Sinatra (see page 46) and Jim Morrison (see page 63) both swore by it. In season 6 of *The Sopranos,* "Bobby Bacala" Baccalieri mixes up a batch to serve as the hair of the dog after a seriously bad fight. As Warren Bobrow says in *The Craft Cocktail Compendium* (2017): "Designed to heal the adverse effects of late nights without doing damage to sensitive stomachs, [the Ramos Fizz] is a powerful emulsifier for maladies of the belly and your aching head (orange flower water has been known to ease headaches and calm jazzy nerves). If you're really feeling rough, get someone else to shake the cocktail for you; remember, no sudden movements." And if you're really, *really* feeling rough, why not use that leftover egg yolk for a Prairie Oyster? Not to be confused with a Rocky Mountain Oyster, the Prairie Oyster has eased the hangovers of literary characters from Bertie Wooster to James Bond. As Jeeves says, "Gentlemen have told me they have found it extremely invigorating after a late evening." If you add a shot of whiskey to make it an Amber Moon, you're on your own.

**1 egg yolk**
**1 teaspoon Worcestershire sauce**
**2 dashes hot sauce**
**Pinch of salt**
**Pinch of pepper**

Put the egg yolk in a juice glass and doctor it with the other ingredients, being careful not to break the yolk.

Drink in one gulp and then sip the Fizz.

Incidentally, this combination was anticipated in 1900, in George Kappeler's *Modern American Drinks,* which offered these instructions for an "Electric Current Fizz": "Make a silver fizz; save the yolk of the egg and serve it in the half-shell, with a little pepper, salt, and vinegar, with the fizz."

# NEW ORLEANS GIN FIZZ FROM THE SAVOY HOTEL, LONDON

Harry Craddock was probably the best-known of a generation of bartenders who left the United States during Prohibition. In 1920 Craddock moved from New York to London, where he became head bartender at the Savoy Hotel's American Bar. His *Savoy Cocktail Book*, published in 1930 and still in print, includes this recipe for a "New Orleans Gin Fizz" (with capitalization unchanged):

**The Juice of ½ Lemon**

**½ Tablespoonful Powdered [i.e., finely ground] Sugar**

**The White of 1 Egg**

**1 Glass [probably 2 ounces] of Dry Gin**

**3 Dashes Fleur d'Orange**

**1 Tablespoonful of Sweet Cream**

Shake well [presumably with ice], strain into long tumbler, and fill with syphon soda water.

# THE CADILLAC BAR'S RAMOS GIN FIZZ

During Prohibition and for years after that, Ramos Gin Fizzes and New Orleans food were on offer just across the border at Nuevo Laredo's Cadillac Bar (see page 38). This recipe is courtesy of Texas journalist Wanda Garner Cash, the founder's granddaughter and author of *Pancho Villa's Saddle at the Cadillac Bar.*

**2 ounces gin**
**2 tablespoons milk**
**1 tablespoon fresh lime juice**
**3 or 4 drops orange blossom water**
**1 heaping tablespoon finely ground sugar**
**1 egg white**
**Seltzer**

Combine all ingredients except the seltzer in a shaker and shake without ice for 1 or 2 minutes.

Add ice and "shake like there's no tomorrow" for a minimum of 5 minutes. (Bartenders say shake until the mixture starts to feel "ropy," whatever that means.)

Strain into a Collins or highball glass and top with a little seltzer.

At the Cadillac, customers got the tall glass, with the shaker and whatever was left on the side.

# HUEY LONG'S RECIPE

In 1933 a wire service story told how Huey Long, Louisiana's new U.S. senator, was making a name for himself in Washington. It described "the loquacious gentleman from Louisiana coatless and perspiring freely," as he shook up what he claimed was "the original, genuine Ramos' gin fizz of 1914." Long's recipe as given in the story is certainly not the one Sam Guarino used that famous afternoon at the New Yorker Hotel. It contains a *lot* of vanilla extract, which Guarino denied using at all, as well as an ungodly amount of orange flower water and much more dairy than is usual.

**White of 1 egg**
**Juice of 1 lemon**
**Six drops vanilla**
**12 drops orange flower water**
**One jigger of gin [try 1½ ounce]**
**One tablespoon powdered [that is, finely ground] sugar**
**"A large quantity of crushed ice"**
**One glass [probably 2 ounces] of milk and cream [half-and-half?]**

Combine first six ingredients and shake.

Add milk and cream [and presumably ice, and presumably shake some more].

# GOLDEN STATE RAMOS FIZZ

In the mid-1970s a recipe for "Golden State Ramos Fizz" cropped up in newspapers around the country. It was mixed in a blender and sprinkled with nutmeg. It also called for bottled sour mix and allowed vodka instead of gin. This recipe is wrongheaded in so many ways . . .

**1½ ounces gin or vodka**

**2 ounces sour mix**

**2 ounces half-and-half**

**½ teaspoon sugar**

**Dash orange flower water**

**1 egg white (This is the *Chicago Tribune*'s version. Others call for the whole egg.)**

**Grated or ground nutmeg**

Put all ingredients except nutmeg in a blender and process until frothy.

Serve at once, sprinkled with nutmeg.

That nutmeg was apparently a West Coast thing. See the "Alta Mira Special," below.

# RAMOS FIZZ FREEZE

Californians' enthusiasm for the Ramos Fizz sometimes took them in strange directions, as when the *Sacramento Bee* published this recipe, which called for two cups of "bottled ramos [*sic*] fizz mix." I've substituted fresh ingredients here.

SERVES 6–8

**1 cup finely ground sugar**
**1 cup lime juice**
**1 cup lemon juice**
**24 drops orange flower water**
**1 pint heavy cream**
**Gin [try 1½ cups]**
**Mint leaves**

Combine the sugar, citrus juice, and orange flower water in mixer bowl or food processor.

Add the cream and beat or process until thick and frothy.

Place in a freezer bowl, cover, and put in freezer for at least 8 hours.

Scoop into individual bowls and drizzle each with 1 tablespoon of gin.

Garnish with mint leaves and serve immediately.

# ALTA MIRA SPECIAL

In 1979 a crack investigative reporter for the *San Francisco Examiner* assayed the Ramos Fizzes at ten bars in San Francisco and Marin County and asked the question, where's the Beefeater? Although nearly all Ramos recipes yield an alcohol content greater than 6 percent, none of the ten Fizzes sampled reached that level. The average was a mere 3.1 percent, and the ones at Sam's Anchor Café in Tiburon and the Alta Mira Hotel in Sausalito apparently contained no gin at all. The *Examiner* had earlier described Sam's as "truly glorified," adding, "Their barmen blend the classic drink to perfection and it's a perfect way to greet a Sunday morning before having their eggs benedict." Sam's only punishment was embarrassment, but the Alta Mira had to pay Marin County five thousand dollars in penalties. Its mistake was to list gin as an ingredient on its cocktail napkins, which was taken to be false advertising. Here's what the napkins said:

**Alta Mira Special**

**Ramos Gin Fizz**

**1½ oz Gin**

**1 Egg White**

**Juice of ½ Lemon**

**2 tsp Sugar**

**3 drops Orange Flower Water**

**½ oz Orange Curacao**

**3 oz Half & Half Cream (light cream in East)**

Place ingredients into blender with small amount of shaved ice. Strain into chimney glass, dust with nutmeg and serve.

In an epic 1979 rant, *San Francisco Examiner* columnist Herb Caen asked, "What's all this to-do over the drink called a Ramos Fizz?" Among his complaints was that "the Ramos comes 'sprinkled with nutmeg.' Nutmeg is the stuff they use to ruin creamed spinach."

# VEGAN FIZZ

All right, I mentioned this earlier, on page 105. But (just curious) if you're a vegan, why are you reading this?

Anyway, obviously you can veganize any Ramos or Ramos-like Fizz by swapping out the egg white and the cream. The going egg-white substitute is the liquid from a can of chickpeas, known in vegan circles as aquafaba (which sounds more appetizing than bean juice). Buy low- or no-sodium chickpeas, shake the can, and drain. Two tablespoons are equivalent to one egg white, and, believe it or not, it behaves like egg white when beaten or shaken, especially with a smidge of cream of tartar. Some say it smells like wet dog, but others deny this; certainly it may have some salinity that has to be ignored. The usual substitute for cream is coconut milk, which does impart a tinge of coconut flavor to the drink, but that's not unpleasant.

In short, it's easy to make a vegan "Ramos Fizz" that's only a little odd and gives the general idea. But M. Carrie Allan, cocktail writer for the *Washington Post,* took a boldly different approach. She masked the salinity and coconut taste by replacing the gin with Scotch whiskey and pineapple juice, which is more than just a *little* odd.

**2 ounces blended Scotch**

**2 tablespoons fresh pineapple juice**

**1 tablespoon fresh lemon juice**

**½ tablespoon simple syrup**

**2 tablespoons coconut milk**

**1½ tablespoons liquid from canned chickpeas**

**2 drops vanilla extract**

**2 dashes Angostura bitters**

**Ice**

**Seltzer**

Put all ingredients except ice and seltzer in a shaker and shake for at least two minutes.

Add ice and shake for 15 seconds.

Strain into glass and top up with seltzer.

If you just want to try a Scotch-based version of a Ramos Fizz and don't care about the vegan part, substitute an egg white for the chickpea liquid and replace the coconut milk with two tablespoons of heavy cream and another half tablespoon of simple syrup.

# CALIFORNIAFIED RAMOS GIN FIZZ

It wasn't just nutmeg that put Herb Caen in a bad mood [see page 123]. He added, "I mean, who cares about New Orleans drinks around here? Anything made with sugar, eggs and cream has to be bad for you, with or without the gin. . . . Stick to San Francisco drinks and live longer." [His "San Francisco drinks" included the Martini, the Bloody Mary, the Mimosa, Anchor Steam Beer, and Fernet-Branca.]

Caen might have been placated by the sort of health-food Ramos Fizz that San Francisco bartender Duggan McDonnell came up with when Amanda Hesser of the *New York Times* asked him to "reinvent" the drink. McDonnell denied setting out to produce "a kind of diet Ramos gin fizz," but, he acknowledged, "that's sort of what it is."

**2 ounces gin [ideally low-proof—e.g., Plymouth]**

**3 ounces milk [2 percent]**

**1 small egg white [or 1 large egg white less 1 teaspoon]**

**2 tablespoons lemon juice**

**1 teaspoon orange marmalade [the bitterest you can find]**

**1½ tablespoons agave nectar syrup [1 part agave nectar to 1 part water]**

**Ice**

**Seltzer**

Put all ingredients except ice and seltzer in a shaker and shake for at least 2 minutes.

Add ice and shake for 15 seconds.

Strain into glass and top up with seltzer.

# FERNET RAMOS

Fernet-Branca [pronounced Fair-net-Brahn-ka] was originally concocted in 1845 in Milan as an anticholera medicine. The recipe is a closely guarded secret, but it's known to contain twenty-seven herbs and spices, from aloe to zedoary. It's an acquired taste, and not everyone acquires it: its flavor has been described as "aggressive, . . . almost like bitter black licorice," "a cross between medicine, crushed plants, and bitter mud," and "like Vicks Vaporub." A character in Cormac McCarthy's novel *The Passenger* observes, "Anything that tastes like this has got to be good for you."

In the 1980s some Argentine college kids started drinking Fernet-Branca and Coca-Cola; now somehow Fernet con Coca has become the national drink of Argentina. On SeriousEats.com, food blogger Lisa Fain ["HomeSickTexan"] says that "the bittersweet, mentholy stuff enhances the spice inherent in Coca-Cola, adding intrigue to the mix like tangling legs of tango dancers." It's a thought.

Around the turn of the twenty-first century, starting in San Francisco, a quick shot of Fernet-Branca came to be called "the Bartender's Handshake," an after-work ritual and a mark of insidership, so perhaps it was inevitable that some craft bartender would try to combine Fernet-and-Coke with the Ramos Fizz. Sure enough, Camille Razo of the Patterson House in Nashville did it. Here's a simplified adaptation of her recipe.

**2 tablespoons Fernet-Branca**

**2 tablespoons blended Scotch**

**2 teaspoons lemon juice**

**2 teaspoons lime juice**

**1½ tablespoons simple syrup**

**3 drops vanilla extract**

**1½ tablespoons orange cordial (see note below)**

**2 tablespoons heavy cream**

**1 egg white**

**Ice**

**3 ounces Coca-Cola (ideally Mexican, with cane sugar)**

Put all ingredients except the ice and Coca-Cola in a shaker and shake well for 3 minutes.

Add ice and shake for one minute.

Pour the Coca-Cola into a Collins glass, then strain the contents of the shaker over the cola. (If you have mix left over in the shaker, set it aside.)

Put the glass in the freezer for three minutes.

Remove the glass from the freezer and *slowly* add any mixture remaining in the shaker.

**NOTE:** You'll only need 1½ tablespoons of orange cordial, but to make the better part of a cup, macerate the peel of one orange in 7 tablespoons of sugar overnight. Remove the peel and combine the sugar with ⅔ cup of orange juice and 2 tablespoons plus 2 teaspoons of lemon juice.

# BOMB TO A GUN FIGHT

This crafty take on the Ramos Fizz by Toby Maloney of the Violet Hour in Chicago calls for not only a particular gin, but a particular brand of bitters and a flavored syrup that you make yourself. Maloney explains, "The gunpowder green tea simple syrup adds complexity, and the hopped bitters add a whiff of cannabis." I'm going to let this represent scores of other variations that require you to seek out exotic ingredients or concoct your own. The "bomb" part is fun.

**2 ounces Ransom Old Tom Gin**

**1 tablespoon fresh lime juice**

**1 tablespoon fresh lemon juice**

**2 tablespoons gunpowder green tea simple syrup (see note below)**

**2 tablespoons heavy cream**

**1 egg white**

**5 drops Bittermens Hopped Grapefruit Bitters**

**1½ ounces soda water**

Shake all ingredients (except soda water) without ice for one minute.

Add ice and shake vigorously for four minutes.

Strain into a pint glass.

Drop in a shot glass of soda water.

**NOTE:** To make ½ cup of gunpowder green tea simple syrup, add 1 ounce of freshly ground gunpowder green tea to ½ cup of room-temperature simple syrup. Let sit for 25 to 30 minutes. Strain and refrigerate.

# RAMOS GIN TOAST

Someone once observed that a Ramos Gin Fizz has the same ingredients as French toast—just up the egg white content a bit, and . . . Well, why not? Another way to have gin for breakfast.

The March 31, 2022, issue of *Garden & Gun* magazine contains Katherine Cobb's recipe for Ramos Gin Fizz Fried Chicken.

You can use just about any kind of white bread for this. Challah is good, but plain sandwich loaf is fine. The bread should be stale: let the slices sit out overnight.

**4 slices stale white bread**

***For the custard:***

**Whites of 4 eggs**
**2 tablespoons heavy cream**
**3 drops orange flower water**
**2 teaspoons fresh lime juice**
**2 teaspoons fresh lemon juice**
**2 drops vanilla**
**Pinch of salt (optional)**

***For the syrup:***

**¼ cup gin**
**½ cup 2:1 simple syrup (see note below)**

Combine gin and syrup. Set aside.

Place custard ingredients in a Mason jar and shake to combine. Put in shallow dish or bowl.

Melt a tablespoon of butter in a large skillet over medium-high heat.

Swirl the bread slices in the custard, one at a time, for a few seconds on each side. Don't let them get soggy, but be sure the custard has soaked in.

Cook two slices at a time until golden brown, 1½ to 2 minutes per side. Refresh butter as needed.

Serve hot with syrup.

**NOTE:** You can substitute commercial cane syrup or even golden syrup for the simple syrup.

---

Dr. George R. Tabor, who is here from Oklahoma City, holds that a Ramos fizz is not a drink, but a food. He took aboard a couple for breakfast today instead of the customary ham and eggs, and he insists that he is not a drinking man at all, but only a seeker after pleasant nourishment.

—*OKLAHOMA NEWS*, reporting from Shreveport (1936)

# SOURCES AND ACKNOWLEDGMENTS

## SELECTED BOOKS CONSULTED

Arthur, Stanley Clisby. *Famous New Orleans Drinks and How to Mix 'Em.* Harmanson, 1937.

Beebe, Lucius. *The Stork Club Bar Book.* Rinehart, 1946.

Bobrow, Warren. *The Craft Cocktail Compendium: Contemporary Interpretations and Inspired Twists on Time-Honored Classics.* Fair Winds, 2017.

Bodenheimer, Neal, and Emily Timberlake. *Cure: New Orleans Drinks and How to Mix 'Em from the Award-Winning Bar.* Abrams, 2022.

Caiafa, Frank. *The Waldorf Astoria Bar Book.* Penguin, 2016.

Cash, Wanda Garner. *Pancho Villa's Saddle at the Cadillac Bar.* Texas A&M University Press, 2020.

DeGroff, Dale. *The Essential Cocktail: The Art of Mixing Perfect Drinks.* Clarkson Potter, 2008.

Egerton, John. *Southern Food: At Home, on the Road, in History.* University of North Carolina Press, 1993.

Grimes, William. *Straight Up or On the Rocks: The Story of the American Cocktail.* Farrar, Straus & Giroux, 2001.

Martin, Ti Adelaide, and Lally Brennan. *In the Land of Cocktails: Recipes and Adventures from the Cocktail Chicks*. William Morrow Cookbooks, 2007.

McMillian, Chris, and Elizabeth Williams. *Lift Your Spirits: A Celebratory History of Cocktail Culture in New Orleans*. Louisiana State University Press, 2016.

Milam, Sara Camp, and Jerry Slater. *The Southern Foodways Alliance Guide to Cocktails*. University of Georgia Press, 2017.

Moss, Robert. *Southern Spirits: Four Hundred Years of Drinking in the American South, with Recipes*. Ten Speed, 2016.

Reed, John Shelton. *Dixie Bohemia: A French Quarter Circle in the 1920s*. Louisiana State University Press, 2012.

Simonson, Robert. *A Proper Drink: The Untold Story of How a Band of Bartenders Saved the Civilized Drinking World*. Ten Speed, 2016.

Washburne, George R., and Stanley Bronner, eds. *Beverages De Luxe*. Wine and Spirit Bulletin, 1911.

Wondrich, David. *Imbibe! From Absinthe Cocktail to Whiskey Smash, a Salute in Stories and Drinks to "Professor" Jerry Thomas, Pioneer of the American Bar*. Rev. ed. TarcherPerigee, 2015.

Wondrich, David, and Noah Rothbaum, eds. *The Oxford Companion to Spirits and Cocktails*. Oxford University Press, 2022.

* * *

Footnotes aren't appropriate for a nonacademic book like this, but in the text I have tried at least to indicate where most direct quotations came from. If this sometimes makes for clunky reading, blame *The Chicago Manual of Style*. In a scholarly work I'd note that Ramos's arrest for violating the Sunday-closure law was reported in the *Times-Democrat* for December 9, 1907; his father's Confederate military record is online at LAAHGP.GenealogyVillage.com; and so forth. But here I'll just say that the vast majority of this material can be found in newspapers and periodicals searchable at Newspapers.com, GenealogyBank.com, and Archive.org (the Internet Archive). Much of the rest came from periodicals and books acquired through the priceless Interlibrary Loan service of the University Library at the University of North Carolina at Chapel Hill. I'm also in debt to the Culinary Institute of America and the New York Public Library for their online menu collections, and to the Exposition Universelle des Vins et Spiritueux for their amazing recipe book library at EUVS-Vintage-Cocktail-Books.cld.bz. I'm grateful to all of these institutions, especially those that don't require a subscription.

Thanks also to the following for help, or at least encouragement: Lee Sioles, late of the LSU Press, for getting me into this project in the first place and for invaluable help with turning the manuscript into a book. Charlie Ramos for everything from telling me how to pronounce his family name to looking at documents for me. The City Archives & Special Collections section of the New Orleans Public Library and the Office of the Orleans Parish Clerk of Civil District Court for help locating legal documents. Wanda Garner Cash for information about her grandfather's Cadillac Bar. Eric Seiferth at the Historic New Orleans Collection. My barbecue buddy Robert Moss, who also knows a thing or two about cocktails. Simon Difford of the splendid diffordsguide.com. Morris Chen for Chinese translation. Cousin Kevin Anderson for incidental research assistance. William L. Selm for information on German Americans in Indiana. Andrew, bartender at the Bourbon Orleans Hotel, for locating the H. C. Ramos cutout. John and Gee Powell for Southern hospitality on Royal Street. Chris McMillian, proprietor of Revel, historian, and raconteur, for graciously sharing his extensive knowledge, his documents, and his illustrations. Cocktail historian Mickey Lyons, for information about shaking machines. Philip Greene, trademark lawyer and cocktail historian. Chris Hannah of Jewel of the South. Duggan

McDonnell, M. Carrie Allan, Camille Razo, and Toby Maloney for their imaginative riffs on the classic. My Jackson friend Suzanne Marrs and Nan Prince of the Mississippi Department of Archives & History. Jenny Keegan and Catherine Kadair at LSU Press, and Susan Murray, my tactful copy editor. And last, but far from least, my wife, Linda, for her good-humored toleration of a yearlong obsession.

At the Bourbon Orleans Hotel, 2023. Linda Miller for Dixie Pix.

John Shelton Reed has written a score of books, innumerable articles, and a few country songs on topics ranging from Southern food to the Church of England. One of his books is *Dixie Bohemia: A French Quarter Circle in the 1920s.* He has been chancellor of the Fellowship of Southern Writers and is cofounder and éminence gris of the Campaign for Real Barbecue. This is his first stab at cocktail writing.

## ICONIC NEW ORLEANS COCKTAILS

*The Sazerac*

*The Café Brûlot*

*The Vieux Carré*

*The Absinthe Frappé*

*The French 75*

*The Roffignac*

*The Brandy Milk Punch*

*The Ramos Gin Fizz*

*The Obituary Cocktail*